Holiday and Seasonal Ideas
for Ministry with Young Teens

HELP

Heads-up | Easy | Low-Cost | Purposeful

Holiday and Seasonal Ideas
for Ministry with Young Teens

Carole Goodwin and Marilyn Kielbasa

HELP

Heads-up | Easy | Low-Cost | Purposeful

Saint Mary's Press
Christian Brothers Publications
Winona, Minnesota

Genuine recycled paper with 10% post-consumer waste.
Printed with soy-based ink.

The publishing team included Marilyn Kielbasa, development editor; Cheryl Drivdahl, copy editor; Barbara Bartelson, production editor; Hollace Storkel, typesetter; Cindi Ramm, art director; Kenneth Hey, cover and logo designer; cover images, PhotoDisc Inc.; produced by the graphics division of Saint Mary's Press.

The development consultants for the HELP (Heads-up, Easy, Low-Cost, and Purposeful) series included the following people:

Sarah Bush, Pewee Valley, Kentucky
Jeanne Fairbanks, Tipp City, Ohio
Carole Goodwin, Louisville, Kentucky
Joe Grant, Louisville, Kentucky
Maryann Hakowski, Belleville, Illinois

Jo Joy, Temple, Texas
Kevin Kozlowski, New Carlisle, Ohio
Jennifer MacArthur, Cincinnati, Ohio
David Nissen, Cincinnati, Ohio
Ruthie Nonnenkamp, Prospect, Kentucky

The activities in this book were created by the authors and by the following contributors:

Joe Grant
Maryann Hakowski

Jo Joy
Ruthie Nonnenkamp

The acknowledgments continue on page 135.

Printed in the United States of America

Printing: 9 8 7 6 5 4 3 2 1

Year: 2008 07 06 05 04 03 02 01 00

ISBN 0-88489-605-6

Library of Congress Cataloging-in-Publication Data

Goodwin, Carole
Holiday and seasonal ideas for ministry with young teens / Carole Goodwin and Marilyn Kielbasa.
       p. cm. — (HELP)
ISBN 0-88489-605-6
1. Church work with teenagers—Catholic Church. 2. Church year—Study and teaching. I. Kielbasa, Marilyn. II. Title. III. HELP (Series : Winona, Minn.)
BX2347.8.Y7 G66 2000
259'.23—dc21
                                                                                          99-050825

Contents

Introduction

Holiday and Seasonal Ideas for Ministry with Young Teens is one of seven books in the HELP series—a collection of **H**eads-up, **E**asy, **L**ow-Cost, and **P**urposeful activities for young adolescents. These strategies are designed to be used as part of a comprehensive youth ministry program for grades six to eight. The strategies can stand alone or complement a religious education curriculum.

The other books in the HELP series are as follows:

◎ *Community-Building Ideas for Ministry with Young Teens* (available in 2001)
◎ *Family Ideas for Ministry with Young Teens*
◎ *Hands-on Ideas for Ministry with Young Teens* (available in 2001)
◎ *Justice and Service Ideas for Ministry with Young Teens*
◎ *Prayer Ideas for Ministry with Young Teens*
◎ *Retreat Ideas for Ministry with Young Teens* (available in 2001)

These books are helpful resources for anyone who works with young adolescents in a church or school setting. They can provide a strong foundation for a year-round, total youth ministry program whose goal is to evangelize young adolescents and support them in their faith journey.

Overview of This Book

Holiday and Seasonal Ideas for Ministry with Young Teens may be used by a coordinator of youth ministry, a director of religious education, catechists, teachers, a parish youth ministry team, or any adult who works with young teens. Ownership of the book includes permission to duplicate any part of it for use with program participants.

The book's strategies are organized according to the calendar year. Secular holidays are represented, as well as holy days and seasons of the liturgical year.

Included are ways to foster learning, engage young teens in service, build community, and attend to the spiritual needs of young adolescents.

Format of the Strategies

Each strategy begins with a brief description of its purpose. The next element is a suggested time for the activity. This is flexible and takes into account several variables, such as the size of the group, the comfort level of the participants, and whether you want to include a break. Use the suggested time as a starting point and modify it according to your circumstances. It is a good idea to include time for a break within the longer strategies.

Next is a description of the size of the group that the strategy was written for. Most of the strategies work with a range of group sizes. If your group is large, be sure to recruit enough adults to help with logistics and supervision. A good rule to follow is that for every six to eight young teens, one adult should be present.

In some strategies a section on special considerations follows the one on group size. It includes things such as notices about remote preparation requirements and cautions to pay special attention to a particular developmental issue of early adolescence.

A complete checklist of materials needed is the next part of the presentation of every strategy. A detailed description of the strategy's procedure is then provided, followed by alternative approaches. Those alternatives may be helpful in adapting the strategy to the needs of your group. In some cases they include a suggestion for reworking the strategy so that it can be used at any time of the year.

Frequently included is a list of scriptural passages that may be used with the strategy for reflection or prayer. The list is not exhaustive; a Bible concordance will provide additional citations if you want to add a more substantial scriptural component to a strategy.

The final element in each strategy offers space for keeping notes about how you might want to use the strategy in the future or change it to fit the needs of your group.

Programming Ideas

The strategies in this book can be used in a variety of ways. Consider the following suggestions:

◎ The program coordinator, catechists, teachers, and coordinator of youth ministry may collaborate to plan youth meetings and special activities that use strategies from this and other books in the HELP series.

◎ Some of the strategies in this book may be used anytime during the year, either as they are presented or with suggested adaptations. Those activities may be presented in the summer months, when most young adolescents are less busy and may be open to a variety of activities. Youth ministers may use those strategies as part of a strong summer program for young teens.

◎ Schoolteachers may use ideas from this and other books in the HELP series to supplement their day-to-day curriculum.

◎ Many of the strategies in the HELP series can be adapted for use with multi-generational groups.

Standard Materials

Many of the items in the materials checklists are common to several strategies in the series. To save time consider gathering frequently used materials in convenient bins and storing those bins in a place that is accessible to all staff and volunteer leaders. Some recommendations for how to organize such bins follow.

Supply Bin

The following items frequently appear in materials checklists:

◎ Bibles, at least one for every two participants
◎ masking tape
◎ cellophane tape
◎ washable and permanent markers (thick and thin)
◎ pens or pencils
◎ self-stick notes
◎ scissors
◎ newsprint
◎ blank paper, scrap paper, and notebook paper
◎ postcards
◎ notepaper
◎ envelopes
◎ baskets
◎ candles and matches
◎ items to create a prayer space (e.g., a colored cloth, a cross, a bowl of water, and a vase for flowers)

Craft Bin

Many of the strategies use craft activities to involve the young people. Consider collecting the following supplies in a separate bin:

◎ construction paper
◎ yarn and string, in assorted colors
◎ poster board
◎ glue and glue sticks

◎ fabric paints
◎ glitter and confetti
◎ used greeting cards
◎ beads
◎ modeling clay
◎ paintbrushes and paints
◎ crayons
◎ used magazines and newspapers
◎ hole punches
◎ scissors
◎ stickers of various kinds
◎ index cards
◎ gift wrap and ribbon

Music Bin

Young people often find deep and profound meaning in the music and lyrics of songs, both past and present. Also, the right music can set an appropriate mood for a prayer or activity. Begin with a small collection of tapes or CDs in a music bin and add to it over time. You might ask the young people to put some of their favorite music in the bin. The bin might include the following styles of music:

◎ *Fun gathering music that is neither current nor popular with young teens.* Ideas are well-known classics (e.g., *Overture to William Tell, Stars and Stripes Forever,* and *1812 Overture*), songs from musical theater productions, children's songs, and Christmas songs for use any time of the year.

◎ *Prayerful, reflective instrumental music, such as the kind that is available in the adult alternative, or New Age, section of music stores.* Labels that specialize in this type of music include Windham Hill and Narada.

◎ *Popular songs with powerful messages.* If you are not well versed in popular music, ask the young people to offer suggestions.

◎ *The music of contemporary Christian artists.* Most young teens are familiar with Amy Grant, Michael W. Smith, and Steven Curtis Chapman. Also include the work of Catholic musicians, such as David W. Kauffman, Steve Angrisano, Bruce Deaton, Sarah Hart, Jesse Manibusan, and Jessica Alles.

Other Helpful Resources

In addition to the seven books in the HELP series, the following resources can be useful in your ministry with young adolescents. All the books in the following list are published by Saint Mary's Press and can be obtained by calling or writing us at the phone number and address listed in the "Your Comments or Suggestions" section at the end of this introduction.

The Catholic Youth Bible, edited by Brian Singer-Towns (2000). The most youth-friendly Bible for Catholic teens available. The scriptural text is accompanied by hundreds of articles to help young people pray, study, and live the Scriptures.

Faith Works for Junior High: Scripture- and Tradition-Based Sessions for Faith Formation, by Lisa-Marie Calderone-Stewart (1993). A series of twelve active meeting plans on various topics related to the Scriptures and church life.

Guided Meditations for Junior High: Good Judgment, Gifts, Obedience, Inner Blindness, by Jane E. Ayer (1997). Four guided meditations for young teens, available on audiocassette or compact disc. A leader's guide includes the script and programmatic options. Other volumes in this series, called A Quiet Place Apart, will also work with young teens.

Looking Past the Sky: Prayers by Young Teens, edited by Marilyn Kielbasa (1999). A collection of 274 prayers by and for young adolescents in grades six to eight.

One-Day Retreats for Junior High Youth, by Geri Braden-Whartenby and Joan Finn Connelly (1997). Six retreats that each fit into a school day or an afternoon or evening program. Each retreat contains a variety of icebreakers, prayers, group exercises, affirmations, and guided meditations.

Prayers with Pizzazz for Junior High Teens, by Judi Lanciotti (1996). A variety of creative prayer experiences that grab young teens' attention. The prayers are useful in many different settings, such as classes, meetings, prayer services, and retreats.

ScriptureWalk Junior High: Bible Themes, by Maryann Hakowski (1999). Eight 90-minute sessions to help bring youth and the Bible together. Each session applies biblical themes to the life issues that concern young teens.

Catechism Connection for Teens collection, by Lisa Calderone-Stewart and Ed Kunzman (1999).

That First Kiss and Other Stories
My Wish List and Other Stories
Better Than Natural and Other Stories
Straight from the Heart and Other Stories
Meeting Frankenstein and Other Stories

The five books in this collection contain short, engaging stories for teens on the joys and struggles of adolescent life, each story with a reflection connecting it to a Catholic Christian belief. Each book's faith connections reflect teachings from a different part of the *Catechism of the Catholic Church.*

Connections to the Discovering Program

The Discovering Program, published by Saint Mary's Press, is a religious education program for young people in grades six to eight. It consists of fourteen six-session minicourses. Each session is 1 hour long and based on the principles of active learning.

The strategies in the HELP series cover themes that are loosely connected to those explored by the Discovering Program, and can be used as part of a total youth ministry program in which the Discovering curriculum is the central catechetical component. However, no strategy in the series presumes that the participants have taken a particular course in the Discovering Program, or requires that they do so. The appendices at the end of this book list the connections between the HELP strategies and the Discovering courses.

Your Comments or Suggestions

Saint Mary's Press wants to know your reactions to the strategies in the HELP series. We are also interested in new youth ministry strategies for use with young teens. If you have a comment or suggestion, please write the series editor, Marilyn Kielbasa, at 702 Terrace Heights, Winona, MN 55987-1320; call the editor at our toll-free number, 800-533-8095; or e-mail the editor at *mkielbasa@smp.org*. Your ideas will help improve future editions of these books.

Getting a Fresh Start
A Reflection Activity on New Year's Resolutions

This reflection activity gives the young people a chance to make a concrete resolution for the New Year and to create a symbol that represents that resolution.

Suggested Time

About 10 minutes

Group Size

This strategy can be done with any size group.

Materials Needed

- 3-by-5-inch index cards, one for each person
- pens or pencils
- envelopes, one for each person
- colored pencils or thin-line markers

PROCEDURE

1. Invite the young people to consider an area of their life that needs improvement. For example, some may need to work harder in school or use more loving behavior in a family relationship. Others might want to improve their relationship with God, such as by praying more often or paying better attention to the liturgy.

2. Give each person one 3-by-5-inch index card, a pen or pencil, and an envelope. Make colored pencils or thin-line markers available to everyone. Tell the young people that they are to write on their card a resolution for improving the area of their life that they have just considered. Then on the other side of the card, they are to draw a symbol that illustrates the resolution. For example, they might sketch a math book or a simple addition problem if their area needing improvement is academics, or a heart to symbolize the need for more loving behavior in a family relationship.

3. When the young people finish drawing, have them place their card in their envelope and write their name on the front of the envelope. Comment briefly that change is difficult and takes patience and persistence, but is always possible. Note that the support of other people is crucial in our efforts to become better people.

4. Close with the following prayer or with one you create spontaneously on the same theme:

O God, send your Holy Spirit to guide us as we face the challenges of making a fresh start. Bless our efforts and help us to remember that we are not alone. We have the support of one another and the guidance of your Spirit. In the name of Jesus, we pray. Amen.

5. Collect the participants' envelopes and save them for at least one month. After that time distribute the envelopes to the young people to remind them of their resolutions and give them an opportunity to assess their progress.

ALTERNATIVE APPROACHES

- In step 3 instruct the young people to write their complete address on their envelope. A month later, instead of distributing the envelopes personally, mail them to the young people.
- Use this activity as part of a New Year reconciliation service, giving the young people a chance to reflect on their actions of the past year and to resolve to improve in the coming year.
- Resolutions can be made at any time of the year. Consider doing this activity as part of a kickoff for a new school year instead of a new calendar year, or for any time you want to talk about new beginnings.

SCRIPTURAL CONNECTIONS

◎ Ezek. 14:6 (Turn yourselves to God.)

◎ Acts 3:19–20 (Reform your lives and turn to God.)

◎ 2 Cor. 5:17–21 (We are made new in Christ Jesus.)

NOTES

Use the space below to jot notes and reminders for the next time you use this strategy.

"I Have a Dream"
A Reflection Exercise on the Speech by Dr. Martin Luther King Jr.

OVERVIEW

In this reflection exercise, the young people hear the words of Dr. Martin Luther King Jr. and each name a dream they have for the future. Then they offer their dreams as part of a prayer litany.

Suggested Time

15 to 20 minutes, depending on the size of the group

Group Size

No more than eight people for each dream catcher

Materials Needed

- a Bible
- copies of handout 1, "'I Have a Dream,'" one for each person
- strips of ribbon, 24 inches long, one for each person
- thin-line permanent markers, one for each person

- 8- to 10-inch embroidery hoops, or wire hangers bent into 8- to 10-inch circles, one for every eight people
- a stapler
- pieces of string, 24 inches long, one for each hoop

PROCEDURE

Preparation. For each group of eight, attach a piece of string to an embroidery hoop or a wire hanger bent into a circle, so that it can be hung from the ceiling or outside in a tree.

1. Read Rev. 21:1–5 to the group. Explain that the writer of the Book of Revelation reflects the same ideas that Jesus expressed when he challenged people to work for a new way of living in community based on the understanding that equality for all is the will of God.

2. Distribute copies of handout 1, with the excerpt from Martin Luther King Jr's. "I Have a Dream" speech. Read the excerpt with your group or invite individuals to take turns reading it. Make the following comments about Dr. King in your own words:

Dr. Martin Luther King Jr. lived when black people were denied basic rights. He challenged them to work for their rights and brought this issue to the forefront of U.S. society.

Dr. King's most famous speech was delivered in front of the Lincoln Memorial in Washington, D.C., on 28 August 1963. He addressed 250,000 people who had demonstrated for the civil rights of black people in the United States. The demonstration was a peaceful one.

Many people consider Dr. King's "I Have a Dream" speech to be his finest speech and one of the best speeches ever delivered by anyone in our country's history.

3. Give each person a strip of ribbon and a thin-line permanent marker. Invite the young people to think about a situation that needs changing in their school, in their community, or in the world. Go around the group and invite each person to state the change he or she thinks needs to happen.

Ask the young people to state their idea in the form of a dream. Have them write their idea on their piece of ribbon, starting with the following words: "I have a dream that one day."

4. When everyone is done writing, read the following prayer:

I have a dream today that we will enjoy a new heaven and a new earth. I have a dream that all God's people will live together in harmony. Let us now pray that all our personal dreams will soon come true. For what other dreams should we now pray?

Invite the young people each to read their dream from their ribbon. After each person reads, instruct her or him to put one end of the ribbon over a hoop and staple it to the rest of the ribbon close to the hoop, creating a streamer. Follow the same process until every person's ribbon is attached to a hoop, putting eight ribbons on each hoop.

5. Hold up the hoops, noting that each young person's dream is now part of a dream catcher filled with prayers. Hang the dream catchers in a prominent place, where everyone in the parish can read the dreams of their young teens.

6. Gather everyone in a circle under the dream catchers. Read Acts 2:17–21, then close with the following prayer:

O God, pour out your Spirit upon us so that we can dream dreams and see visions. We call on your name to help us build a new heaven and a new earth. We ask this in the name of Jesus, who taught us to follow our dreams by following you. And so we say amen.

ALTERNATIVE APPROACHES

◎ Instead of having the young people read the excerpt from Dr. King's speech, get an audiotape or videotape of the actual event and play it for them.
◎ Rather than making group dream catchers, ask the young people each to attach their ribbon to their clothing with a safety pin. Invite them to wear their ribbon on Martin Luther King Jr. Day, as a dream maker for a new way of living.
◎ Provide a large hula hoop and make ribbons and markers available to other members of the parish. Invite everyone in the parish to attach their own dream for a better world.

SCRIPTURAL CONNECTIONS

◎ Ps. 126:1–3 (The Lord has done great things for dreamers.)
◎ Joel 2:28 (They shall dream dreams.)
◎ Rev. 21:1–5 (We shall have a new city.)

NOTES

Use the space below to jot notes and reminders for the next time you use this strategy.

"I Have a Dream"

I HAVE A DREAM that one day this nation will rise up and live out the true meaning of its creed: "We hold these truths to be self-evident; that all men are created equal."

I have a dream that one day, on the red hills of Georgia, sons of former slaves and the sons of former slaveowners will be able to sit down together at a table of brotherhood.

I have a dream that my four little children will one day live in a nation where they will not be judged by the color of their skin but by the content of their character. . . .

I have a dream that one day . . . little black boys and black girls will be able to join hands with little white boys and white girls and walk together as sisters and brothers. . . .

I have a dream that one day "every valley shall be exalted, every hill and mountain shall be made low, the rough places will be made plains, and the crooked places will be made straight, and the glory of the Lord shall be revealed, and all shall see it together." (As quoted in Alex Ayres, editor, *The Wisdom of Martin Luther King, Jr.* [Meridian, 1993], pages 63–64. Copyright © 1993 by Alex Ayres.)

Soup or Bowl

A Game and Service Project for Super Bowl Sunday

OVERVIEW This combination game and service project is played in relay style by teams of young people with cans of soup that they bring as donations for the local food pantry.

Suggested Time

A minimum of 10 minutes, or as long as the group wants to play

Group Size

Six to eight people in small groups, with each small group forming a relay team

Materials Needed

- masking tape
- basketballs, one for each team
- donated cans of soup
- newsprint and markers

PROCEDURE

Preparation. Before the gathering send a message to the participants telling them to bring cans of soup to donate to people who are poor. Mention that the more cans they bring, the more fun they will have at this event.

Create a bowling lane for each group of six to eight people as follows: With masking tape mark a ball line and a pyramid line at opposite ends of the meeting space. Place a basketball on the ball line.

1. Divide the young people into small groups of six to eight people and assign each group a bowling lane. Direct the members of each team to stack the cans of soup they brought into a pyramid on the line you marked earlier. Tell half the members of each team to line up in back of their pyramid. Those people are the stackers. The other half of each team should line up in back of their basketball. Those are the bowlers.

Explain the following rules in your own words:

The person who is first in the bowling line will roll the ball toward the stack of cans. The team gets a point for every can that falls off its pyramid when the ball hits it. Throwing is not allowed. If a bowler throws the ball, the team gets no points.

When the ball hits the stack, the bowler runs to the end of the stacking line. Meanwhile the stackers reset the pyramid as quickly as they can. The pyramid must be stacked the same way every time.

When the pyramid has been restacked, the first person in the stacking line runs to the end of the bowling line. When he or she reaches the line, the next bowler rolls the ball, and the team follows the same process for bowling, stacking, and rotating places. The game continues until you call time.

Keep score on newsprint. The team with the most points at the end of the game wins.

2. After the game donate the cans of soup to a local food pantry.

ALTERNATIVE APPROACHES

◎ Follow the game with a soup supper.
◎ Challenge other groups in the parish or other youth groups to a soup-or-bowl tournament and award prizes to the winners. For the young person who brings the most cans of soup, provide gift certificates to a fast-food restaurant or a bag of snack food. Give the tournament winners plastic soup bowls—blue bowls for the first-place team, red bowls for second place, and yellow bowls for third. End the tournament with a soup supper.
◎ Instead of knocking down cans, use an actual bowling game with pins and balls, and award cans of soup for the top score after each round. Also give prizes to the team with the most cans at the end of the game.

◎ Help the young teens run a soup-or-bowl tournament for young children. You may want to use empty soup cans and soft foam balls for the game itself.

◎ Ask the entire parish to bring cans of soup to Mass on Super Bowl Sunday.

SCRIPTURAL CONNECTIONS

◎ Isa. 58:7 (Share your bread with the hungry.)

◎ Matt. 25:35–40 (I was hungry, and you gave me food.)

◎ James 2:14–17 (Put faith into action.)

NOTES

Use the space below to jot notes and reminders for the next time you use this strategy.

Valentine Visit

An Outreach Event for Valentine's Day

This strategy brings a holiday slant to a standard outreach project—a visit to a nursing home for older people. Such a visit allows the young people to connect with elderly people and also gives them an opportunity to discuss how older people are cared for in the community. You will need one session to prepare for the visit, in addition to the actual visit.

Suggested Time

About 60 minutes for the planning meeting, depending on the number of young people and how elaborate and creative they are with the cards

Group Size

This strategy works best with up to twenty young teens, depending on the number of residents you are visiting.

Special Considerations

Most young people are uncomfortable around nursing home residents. During the planning session, be sure to discuss with the participants things they might encounter in their visit. For example, some of the elderly people will be senile and may not respond in ways the young people expect, some of the residents may be sick, many may look sad and depressed, and many will be unresponsive. Remind the young people that each of the residents is a human person, created by God, cared for by God, and loved by God. Emphasize that all the residents deserve to be treated with respect and dignity.

Materials Needed

- ☼ paper in a variety of colors and types
- ☼ scissors
- ☼ glue
- ☼ markers
- ☼ heart stickers
- ☼ other items that can be used for creating valentine cards, such as doilies, ribbon, yarn, Mylar confetti, and hole punches
- ☼ copies of the lyrics to sing-along songs for the young people and the residents

PROCEDURE

Preparation. Make arrangements to visit a nursing home on or around Valentine's Day. Check with the administration about the guidelines for such visits and the best way to connect with the residents. Get a list of the names of the residents if you can, or at least some idea of the number of residents you will be visiting.

Recruit other adults to transport the young people, and secure the necessary permission forms.

Find the lyrics to songs that the young people know, such as "This Little Light of Mine," "When the Saints Go Marching In," and "Battle Hymn of the Republic." Many sing-along books include lyrics that can be duplicated. Check a music store or your local library.

Planning Meeting

1. When the young people gather, tell them about the nursing home visit and the circumstances they might encounter. Allow them to discuss any anxieties or discomforts they have. Share the following instructions:

Imagine that you are about to meet someone who has lived a long time and has done amazing things. This person may not be able to talk any longer, but she or he probably knows when someone is visiting. Your role is to smile and be friendly and share your presence.

2. Explain the details and logistics of the visit. Assign partners, and tell them that they will travel together and visit the same people and share the experience with each other.

3. Provide paper, scissors, glue, markers, heart stickers, and a wide variety of other art supplies for the young people to use in making valentine cards for the nursing home residents. The cards should be as colorful and festive as possible. Be sure that every resident will get at least one card.

4. Distribute lyrics for sing-along songs the group will lead, and practice the songs. Explain that the young people should invite the residents to join in the singing, but warn them not to be surprised if few do. Note that the older people's lack of active participation should not dampen their own enthusiasm.

5. Help the participants create a group cheer or chant, such as the one that follows. Tell them that they will use this cheer when they arrive at the nursing home or to announce their arrival at each room there. Caution them not to get too boisterous.

> We are here
> to bring you cheer.
> Join our singing,
> our voices bringing
> joy-filled sounds that sing and say
> it is love we share this Valentine's Day!

Valentine Visit

1. On the day of the visit, with the adults you have recruited, help the young people present their cheer or chant, distribute their cards, pass out sing-along lyrics, lead a sing-along, and visit with the residents for as long as time allows.

2. After the visit lead the young people in a discussion of the following questions:

What was the best thing about the visit?

What can you tell the group about someone you met? Share their name and anything you learned about them or from them.

Did anything bother you about the visit?

What could be done to improve the life of the residents?

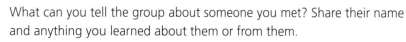

3. Close with the following prayer or one that you create spontaneously:

God of all that is good, stay by the side of the special people we met today. Help them to feel your strength as they face each day. Keep them safe. And may we always remember them in our prayers. We ask this in the name of Jesus. Amen.

ALTERNATIVE APPROACHES

◎ Instead of planning a sing-along, help the young people prepare an appropriate skit to present to the residents.

◎ Encourage the young teens to dress in costumes or as valentine clowns.

◎ In place of gathering sing-along songs, encourage the young people to create "valentine carols" by changing the words of popular Christmas carols to reflect the valentine themes of love, friendship, and care.

◎ Provide the young teens with Bibles and help them look up scriptural verses on the theme of love. Encourage them to add their favorite verse to the cards they make.

◎ Instead of helping the young people create a cheer or chant to use at the nursing home, invite them to write a short prayer asking God's blessings on the residents and on the visit.

NOTES

Use the space below to jot notes and reminders for the next time you use this strategy.

Real Love Is . . .

A Community-Building and Discussion Event for Valentine's Day

OVERVIEW

The five activities in this strategy can be programmed together to create a special event for Valentine's Day or used separately as part of different meetings or classes.

Suggested Time

Up to 90 minutes, depending on the size of the group and whether you include all five activities

Group Size

These activities work best with a group of up to twenty participants. If your group is larger, recruit adults to help.

Materials Needed

- ☼ a large poster board heart
- ☼ masking tape

- thin-line markers
- used magazines
- glue sticks
- pastel candy hearts with sayings on them
- copies of resource 1, "Valentine Bingo," one for each person
- markers or crayons
- prizes (optional)
- poster board hearts, about 6 inches wide, one for every four or five people
- a scissors
- Bibles
- cellophane tape
- blank sheets of paper
- pens or pencils
- a tape or CD player, and a recording of reflective music (optional)
- a basket
- small paper hearts, about 2 inches wide, one for each person
- newsprint

PROCEDURE

Graffiti Heart

Preparation. Purchase a large cardboard heart from a party supply store or make one out of poster board, and post it in an obvious place in the meeting room. Write the words, "Real love is . . . ," at the top of the heart. Place a container of thin-line markers, several used magazines, and a few glue sticks near it. (If your group is large, you may want to post several large hearts or a sheet of butcher paper that is decorated with large hearts.)

As the young people arrive, call their attention to the large heart posted on the wall. Tell them to add to the heart their idea of what love really is. Suggest that they write their idea on the heart, or tear from a magazine a picture or phrase that represents real love and glue it on the heart.

Candy Heart Bingo

Preparation. Purchase a bag of pastel candy hearts with sayings on them such as "Be mine" and "U R #1." Use resource 1, "Valentine Bingo," to create bingo cards by writing phrases from the candy hearts in the open squares. The phrases should be arranged differently on each card. If you do not have enough different phrases to fill in all twenty-four open squares, repeat phrases. You might also leave out some phrases on various cards. Make one card for each participant.

Give each person a bingo card and a marker or crayon. Tell the young people that you will choose a candy heart from the bag and read the phrase on it. They are to put an *X* in the appropriate square if they have that phrase on their card. Note that they are to mark only one square each time a phrase is read, even if the phrase appears in more than one square on their card. The first person to fill in five squares vertically, horizontally, or diagonally is the winner. Note that the middle square has already been filled in for them, with a heart. If you have a prize available, award it to the winner.

Valentine Puzzles

Preparation. Purchase or make a poster board heart, about 6 inches wide, for every four or five young people. Write on each heart a different scriptural verse that pertains to love. Include the citation. Here are some possible citations:

- Deut. 6:5
- Ps. 130:7
- Jer. 31:3
- Matt. 22:39
- John 13:35
- John 15:12
- Rom. 8:35
- 1 Cor. 13:4–5
- Col. 3:14
- 1 John 4:11

Cut each heart into four or five pieces, and mix up the pieces from all the hearts.

Give each participant one of the heart pieces that you have created. Direct the young teens to find the other people whose pieces complete their heart. Make Bibles available to them in case they need to check the wording of a citation. Tell them to tape together their heart when their small group is complete.

Real-Acts-of-Love Calendar

1. Comment that the act of loving people is not restricted to Valentine's Day, and that real love must happen every hour of every day. If you used the Graffiti Heart activity earlier in the session, review the words and pictures that the young teens put on the large heart. Discuss with them how real love differs from some notions about love that come from the media and popular culture.

2. Announce that the participants are going to observe Valentine's Month by creating and using a monthlong calendar with a suggestion for performing an act of real love on each day. (The calendar might span the month of February or the month between February 14 and March 14.) Distribute blank sheets of paper evenly among the groups—one sheet for each day of the month, plus several extra sheets for each group. Also pass out pens or pencils. Direct the groups each to use one of their extra sheets of paper to brainstorm a list of some

acts of real love. You might want to give some examples like the ones that follow:

Secretly do something nice for someone in your family.

Write a note to a teacher, telling the teacher what you appreciate most about her or his class.

Say a prayer for someone who did something wrong.

Give up buying snack food, and put the money you save in the church collection on Sunday.

Explain that after the groups brainstorm their list, they are to decide which ideas are most creative and feasible. They are then to write one of those acts of real love on each sheet of paper.

3. When the small groups have finished their work, organize the papers into a large calendar on the wall or on the floor. Begin by asking the groups to post their best responses, then replace any duplicate suggestions with extra ideas that were generated in the brainstorming sessions.

4. Tell the young teens that they will each get a copy of the calendar so that they can observe Valentine's Month by performing an act of real love every day. Ask for a volunteer to re-create the calendar on 8$\frac{1}{2}$-by-11-inch paper by hand or with a computer, and to copy the acts of real love into the appropriate spaces. When the volunteer completes the task, give or send a copy to everyone in the group.

Valentine Prayer

Preparation. Purchase or make enough small paper hearts for everyone in the class to have one. Put the hearts in a basket.

Write the following statements on a sheet of newsprint. If you used the Graffiti Heart activity earlier in this meeting, post the newsprint near the large heart and cover it.

_____ is always patient and kind.

_____ is never jealous.

_____ is never boastful or conceited.

_____ does not insist on his or her own way.

_____ is not irritable or resentful.

_____ does not keep score of other people's offenses.

_____ always looks for the truth.

_____ is always ready to trust, to believe, to hope, and to face whatever happens.

1. If you used the Graffiti Heart activity earlier in the session, gather all the young teens in front of the large heart. If you have reflective music, begin playing it at this time. If you used the Valentine Puzzles activity earlier in the session, ask someone from each small group to read the scriptural verse from the group's puzzle heart and to post the heart near the gathering. Place a basket with small paper hearts, and pens or pencils, at the front of the gathering.

2. Announce that you are going to read from the Bible a famous passage that explains what real love is. Ask the young people to close their eyes. Then slowly and deliberately, one phrase at a time, read 1 Cor. 13:1–2,4–7,13.

3. Maintaining a mood of reflective silence, pass the basket of hearts, and the pens or pencils, and direct the young people to take one of each.

Display the newsprint that you created before the session, pointing out that it is based on 1 Cor. 13:4–7. Tell the young teens to read each statement silently. In the blank space—where the word *love* appears in the Bible—they are to silently say their own name. Suggest that they think about whether the statement is true with their name inserted in place of *love*. For example, is it true to say, "Lucy is always patient and kind" or "William does not keep score of other people's offenses"?

After a minute of silence for this reflection, direct the young teens to write on their paper heart one thing they need to work on in order to become a person of real love. Tell them to take the heart home and put it where they can see it every day and evaluate their progress.

ALTERNATIVE APPROACHES

◎ To expedite the process of creating bingo cards, gather several people together before the event. Give each person a bingo card made from resource 1, and a pen. Then read the phrases from the candy hearts you have purchased, and direct everyone to write each phrase in a different square. Or follow the same process with all the participants at the beginning of the activity, then have everyone exchange cards for the game.

◎ Guide the young teens in using the bingo game as part of a valentine visit to a nursing home.

◎ Make copies of the real-acts-of-love calendar available to everyone in the parish. You might put copies in the parish bulletin, with an explanation of how and by whom the calendar was created.

◎ Post the large version of the real-acts-of-love calendar on a wall in a parish gathering space. If your group also made a graffiti heart, include it as part of the display.

◉ For the Valentine Prayer activity, instead of writing the verses from First Corinthians on newsprint, use them to create a prayer card for each young teen. Distribute the cards at the end of the session, instructing the participants to write their name in all the blanks and to use the card to evaluate their actions and attitudes periodically.

NOTES

Use the space below to jot notes and reminders for the next time you use this strategy.

Valentine Bingo

Resource 1: Permission to reproduce this resource for program use is granted.

33

Ashes to Reconciliation

A Reconciliation Prayer for Lent

OVERVIEW

This prayer can be used during the first week of Lent or any time the sacrament of Reconciliation (also called the sacrament of Penance) is discussed or celebrated.

Suggested Time

30 to 45 minutes, depending on the size of the group

Group Size

This strategy works best with a group of up to fifteen participants. If your group is larger, recruit adults to help.

Materials Needed

- ☼ a pillar candle and matches
- ☼ 2-by-3-inch pieces of paper, one for each person
- ☼ pens or pencils
- ☼ a Bible
- ☼ empty coffee cans, one for every fifteen people
- ☼ a pitcher of water
- ☼ tin pie pans, one for every fifteen people
- ☼ a tape or CD player, and a recording of reflective music or a Lenten hymn

PROCEDURE

Preparation. Before the young people arrive, set up a prayer space in the middle of your meeting place. It should include a pillar candle (preferably the parish's Easter candle) and matches, a Bible, an empty coffee can for every fifteen people in the group, a pitcher of water, a tin pie pan for every fifteen people, and a tape or CD player set to play a recording of reflective music or a Lenten hymn.

1. Gather the young people in a circle around the prayer space. Light a pillar candle. Distribute a small piece of paper and a pen or pencil to each person, but tell the young teens not to write anything until they are instructed to do so. Ask them to close their eyes and listen as you read Matt. 3:1–3.

2. When you finish reading, tell the young people to keep their eyes closed and invite them to consider in what areas of their life they need to repent or reform and what changes they can make. After a few seconds of silence, read the following examen, pausing briefly for each response from the group:

Leader. For the times we have ignored our classmates who feel lonely or left out, we pray . . .

All. O God, forgive us.

Leader. For the times we have been rude or disrespectful to our parents, teachers, or other adults who care for us, we pray . . .

All. O God, forgive us.

Leader. For the times we have wasted food or taken for granted what we have, we pray . . .

All. O God, forgive us.

Leader. For the times we have used other people for our own pleasure or gain by inappropriate behavior or by gossiping or fighting, we pray . . .

All. O God, forgive us.

Leader. For the times we have put ourselves down, forgetting that we are created in God's image and should reflect that image to all we meet, we pray . . .

All. O God, forgive us.

Leader. For the times we have not paid attention at Mass or during prayer, we pray . . .

All. O God, forgive us.

After a minute or so of silence, tell the young people to write on their piece of paper one thing they will change.

3. Collect all the papers in one or more coffee cans and burn them. (Put no more than fifteen papers in a single can.) Be sure to have a pitcher of water handy in case the flames get too large. Pour the burned ashes from each coffee can into a tin pie pan and stir them around. Allow about 5 minutes for them to cool. While the ashes are cooling, play some quiet reflective music or a Lenten hymn, and invite the young people to listen in silence and think about the change they will be making. If you think your group will find it difficult to handle 5 minutes of silence without something to help them focus, distribute blank paper and ask the young people to write down other changes they hope to make.

4. When the ashes have cooled, take them to each person and ask, "Are you ready to repent, to leave your sinful ways and to follow the Gospel?" After the young person responds, "Yes," make the sign of the cross on his or her forehead with ashes.

5. After all the young people have been marked with ashes, gather the group near the candle, and explain that the candle represents the light of Christ, who came into the world to forgive sins. Read Dan. 9:3–4. Then say the following prayer:

Forgive us, O God, for we have sinned against you and your commandments. May we use your guidance to become more faithful followers of the teachings of Jesus. We ask this in the name of Jesus, who taught us to pray for forgiveness. And so we pray together . . . [Conclude with the Lord's Prayer.]

ALTERNATIVE APPROACHES

◎ Invite a priest to celebrate the sacrament of Reconciliation with the participants before anointing them with ashes.

◎ Before you read the passage from Matthew's Gospel, lead the group to list on poster board or newsprint the ways people their age sin. Display this poster for their reference as they think about the area in their life that needs reform.

SCRIPTURAL CONNECTIONS

◎ Ezek. 18:30–32 (Turn away from sin.)
◎ Matt. 3:1–4 (Reform your life.)
◎ Luke 7:44–50 (Your sins are forgiven.)

NOTES

Use the space below to jot notes and reminders for the next time you use this strategy.

Lenten Nails

A Reflection Exercise for Lent

This two-part reflection exercise allows the young teens to evaluate their behaviors and attitudes and admit their faults, throughout Lent. The exercise is introduced at the beginning of Lent and concludes before Easter.

Suggested Time

Approximately 10 minutes for part A; about 15 minutes for part B, depending on the size of the group

Group Size

This strategy can be done with any size group.

Special Considerations

This strategy happens in two parts. Part A should be scheduled as close to Ash Wednesday as possible. Part B should take place at the end of Lent.

Materials Needed

Part A
- :☼: a hammer
- :☼: a cross or crucifix
- :☼: large and small nails, one of each for each person plus a few extra for display
- :☼: a Bible

Part B
The hammer, cross or crucifix, extra nails for display, and Bible from part A, plus the following items:
- :☼: a basket
- :☼: an empty coffee can
- :☼: matches
- :☼: a pitcher of water
- :☼: a dishpan of sand
- :☼: a large wooden or metal spoon
- :☼: a stick (optional)

PROCEDURE

Part A

Preparation. Before the young people arrive, set up a prayer space in a central location, with a hammer, a cross or crucifix, large and small nails for the participants and for display, and a Bible.

1. Gather the young people in the prayer space. When they are settled, say the following prayer or one that is spontaneous:

 O God, you know what is in our hearts and what is in our thoughts. Help us to examine our lives during this Lenten season and to know that you always forgive the things we do wrong.

2. Give each person a large nail and a small nail. Explain that the young people are to carry the small nail in a pocket all during Lent. When they reach into the pocket and feel the nail, they are to pause for a moment to think about their behaviors and attitudes.

The large nail is to be kept in their room. When they do something wrong, display a negative attitude, or act in a way that hurts themselves or someone else, at any time during the six weeks of Lent, they should write the offense on a piece of paper and attach the paper to the nail. At the end of Lent, they will bring the large nail, with their offenses attached, to the second part of this activity.

Part B

Preparation. A few days before conducting the second part of this activity, remind the young people to bring to the session their large nail with their offenses attached.

Set up a prayer space as you did for part A, minus the nails you have already distributed to the young people.

1. Gather the young people in the prayer space. When they are settled, say the following prayer or one that is spontaneous:

> O God, you know what is in our hearts and what is in our thoughts. We have examined our lives during this Lenten season and know that you forgive all our offenses.

2. Pass a basket around the group. Tell the participants to take the papers off their nail and place them in the basket, saying a prayer of contrition as they do so. When all the papers have been collected, burn them a few at a time in a coffee can, adding them to the fire as the flames diminish. Keep a pitcher of water nearby in case the flames get out of hand. (If you have a large group, you may want to use several coffee cans and recruit adult helpers to speed this process.)

3. When the flames have died, ask one of the participants to mix the ashes into a dishpan of sand, using a large spoon. As the person is doing so, read John 8:3–11, slowly and prayerfully. After you are finished reading, write in the sand with a stick or with your fingertip, "You are forgiven!"

ALTERNATIVE APPROACHES

◎ Consider this option if your group is not too large: Before the young people gather for part A of the strategy, build a simple wooden cross out of two pieces of wood. (Or you could ask one of the young people to build the cross.) Then hammer the nails for the participants partway into the cross so that they can easily be pulled out. Instead of simply distributing the nails during the group meeting, invite the participants each to remove one small and one large nail from the cross.

◎ In the prayer space, use a cross made out of two plain pieces of wood. Instead of passing a basket around the group to collect the offenses in part B, place the basket near the cross. Tell the young people to come forward one at a time, place their papers into the basket, and hammer their nail into the cross.

◎ Instead of offering this strategy in two sessions, at the beginning and end of Lent, combine the parts into one session and use it as a Lenten reconciliation service. You can do this by eliminating the small nails. At the beginning of the service, give each person a large nail, some small pieces of paper, and a pencil. Conduct a brief examination of conscience, then give the young people time to go off by themselves and reflect on their offenses, writing each one on a piece of paper and attaching it to their nail. If a priest is available, offer the option of sacramental Reconciliation.

SCRIPTURAL CONNECTIONS

◎ Ezek. 18:30–32 (Turn away from sin.)
◎ Matt. 3:1–4 (Reform your life.)
◎ Luke 7:44–50 (Your sins are forgiven.)

NOTES

Use the space below to jot notes and reminders for the next time you use this strategy.

Justice Walk

A Contemporary Version of the Stations of the Cross

OVERVIEW This exercise uses the stations of the cross as a backdrop, and applies the meaning of the stations to modern life. The young people walk around their city or town, stopping at various places that are part of life for people who are impoverished, downtrodden, or suffering. The justice walk may take a considerable amount of preparation time, but the effect on young teens can be significant.

Suggested Time

45 to 90 minutes, depending on the number of locations on the walk and the size of the group

Group Size

This strategy can be done with any size group.

Materials Needed

☀ a portable sound system (optional)

PROCEDURE

Preparation. Determine places in your city or town that can serve as a backdrop for this justice walk. Some examples are a jail, homeless shelter, soup kitchen, courthouse, government building, employment office, welfare office, hospital or clinic, cemetery, women's center, and park where homeless people gather. Notify the administrations of those places of your intent. Depending on the size of your group, you may also need to notify the local police about your activity.

Decide how each location connects to one of the stations of the cross, which are listed below. For example, the first station, Jesus is condemned to death, can be related to a jail where people await sentencing. The sixth station, Veronica wipes the face of Jesus, might be particularly applicable to the ministry of people who work in soup kitchens or shelters. For one version of the stations of the cross, see the book *Stations for Teens,* by Gary Egeberg (Winona, MN: Saint Mary's Press, 2000). Ideally, the justice walk will cover fourteen locations, each corresponding to one of the stations of the cross. However, you can conduct the activity with fewer locations.

1. Jesus is condemned to death.
2. Jesus carries his cross.
3. Jesus falls the first time.
4. Jesus meets his mother.
5. Simon of Cyrene helps Jesus carry the cross.
6. Veronica wipes the face of Jesus.
7. Jesus falls the second time.
8. Jesus meets the women of Jerusalem.
9. Jesus falls the third time.
10. Jesus is stripped of his garments.
11. Jesus is nailed to the cross.
12. Jesus dies on the cross.
13. Jesus' body is taken down from the cross.
14. Jesus' body is laid in the tomb.

Arrange transportation for your group to a starting point. If the locations are far apart, you might want to have drivers available to take the young people from place to place as well. Decide on a logical route for the justice walk.

Depending on the size of your group and the noisiness of the locations, you may want to take along a portable sound system that can easily be set up, taken down, and moved from place to place.

1. When the young people gather at the starting point, explain to them the significance of the stations of the cross in the history of Catholic devotions. Mention that since the stations were developed in the Middle Ages, they have provided a way for people to meditate on the Passion and death of Jesus. Note that many people in the world today experience traumatic and painful events that relate to the suffering of Jesus, though they do not experience them in the same ways that Jesus did.

Tell the young teens that they will have a chance to pray for some of those modern-day sufferers. Explain that they will be moving from place to place, stopping at each one to pray for the people whose lives are connected to that place in some way.

2. Move to the first station and announce its name. Play appropriate music if you choose to do so. Say a gathering prayer such as the one that follows, or create one spontaneously:

> *Leader.* God of suffering and compassion, we praise you, we bless you, we honor you.
> *All.* You bring hope to the world.

Discuss with the young people how the work that goes on in this location and its effect on people are related to the station of the cross the location represents. Invite the young teens to speak spontaneous prayers for the people who are in some way affected by the agency or service.

Close with a simple prayer, such as the following one:

> *Leader.* God of justice . . .
> *All.* Have mercy on us.

Follow the same process for the remaining stations.

ALTERNATIVE APPROACHES

◎ For the closing prayer at the end of your visit to a station, you could sing a simple responsive version of the penitential rite (or Rite of Reconciliation) from the Sunday liturgy: "Lord, have mercy; Christ, have mercy; Lord, have mercy."

◎ Involve the young teens from the beginning of the planning process. Invite them to choose the locations based on the stations and to write a prayer for the group to say at each location. You may have to create a print piece to distribute to those who participate in the walk. The young people can help with that task, too.

◎ Open the justice walk to the entire parish community. Either help the young people create and facilitate the event, or recruit various parish groups to take responsibility for one or more stations.

◎ After the walk is completed, gather the group for a simple "poverty" meal of soup or of rice and beans.

SCRIPTURAL CONNECTIONS

The following citations refer you to the Passion narratives in the Gospels:

- Matt. 26:57—27:60
- Mark 15:1–46
- Luke 23:1–53
- John 18:28—19:42

NOTES

Use the space below to jot notes and reminders for the next time you use this strategy.

The Passion Here and Now

A Contemporary Look at the Passion of Jesus Christ

This activity helps the young teens connect the suffering of Jesus with the sufferings of people around the world. It also helps them to become familiar with the Passion narrative in the Gospel of Luke.

Suggested Time

15 to 25 minutes, depending on the size of the group

Group Size

This strategy works well with up to fifteen participants. If you have more than that, you may want to post multiple sheets of newsprint or poster board for each topic heading.

Materials Needed

- :☼: a variety of newspapers and news magazines
- :☼: a scissors
- :☼: six sheets of newsprint or poster board
- :☼: markers
- :☼: masking tape

☼ a Bible
☼ cellophane tape, at least one roll for every three people

PROCEDURE

Preparation. Collect newspaper and magazine articles and photographs that depict tragedies and sufferings of people around the world. Include stories of war, starvation, violence, murder, struggle, serious illness, abuse, and so forth. You will need two or three articles and photographs for each participant.

Write each of the following headlines across the top of a piece of newsprint or poster board and post the finished signs around the room:
◎ Fear and agony
◎ Betrayal and arrest
◎ Denial and abandonment
◎ Judgment in court
◎ Suffering, abuse, and torture
◎ Wrongful death

1. Gather the young people and lead them in the following prayer or a spontaneous prayer on the same theme:

O Jesus, because you suffered, you know what suffering is. We remember your Passion today. As we hear of the plight of people in our world who also suffer and sometimes die a terrible death, may we remember that you need us to have compassion for our brothers and sisters. Guide our actions and the actions of our leaders so that we are not the cause of suffering and death for others. We ask this in your name. Amen.

2. Distribute newspaper articles and photographs about tragedy and suffering, so that each person has two or three. Point out the headlines posted around the room. Tell the young people to read their articles and look at their photographs silently, and to think about which headline each might fall under. Note that they do not have to make a final decision yet.

3. After a few minutes, stand near the first headline and read Luke 22:39–46. Pause at the end of the passage, and then move to the next head-line and read its corresponding passage from Luke. Read each of the remaining sections of Luke's Passion narrative in the same manner. The headlines and their corresponding sections of the narrative are listed below.
◎ Fear and agony (Luke 22:39–46)
◎ Betrayal and arrest (Luke 22:47–53)
◎ Denial and abandonment (Luke 22:54–65)
◎ Judgment in court (Luke 22:66—23:25)
◎ Suffering, abuse, and torture (Luke 23:26–38)
◎ Wrongful death (Luke 23:39–49)

4. After you have read all six passages, tell the young people to match their articles and photographs to the headlines and to tape each one to the appropriate newsprint or poster board. Give them time to look over the completed sheets before gathering them for a closing prayer.

5. Comment on the continued presence of evil and suffering in the world, and the power of human beings to change that reality through prayer and consistent work for justice. Close the activity with this prayer:

Leader. For the leaders of all countries in our world, that they may pass legislation that frees rather than oppresses people, we pray to the Lord.
All. Lord, hear our prayer.

Leader. For those who suffer injustice, who experience agony and abandonment just as Jesus did, we pray to the Lord.
All. Lord, hear our prayer.

Leader. For an end to the violence and corruption that are the daily fare of many people of poverty, we pray to the Lord.
All. Lord, hear our prayer.

Leader. In gratitude for Jesus, who chose freely to come among us and who knows what it is like to suffer, we pray to the Lord.
All. Lord, hear our prayer.

ALTERNATIVE APPROACHES

◎ Instead of supplying individual articles and photos, begin the activity by pointing out the headlines posted around the room. Provide a variety of newspapers and magazines and challenge the young people to find and cut out at least one article or picture applicable to every headline.

◎ If your participants are not likely to sit still for the entire reading of the Passion narrative, pause after each section and allow people time to tape up the articles that pertain to the corresponding headline.

◎ Ask six young people to read the Passion narrative, one for each section. Choose people before the session so that they have a chance to practice reading their passage.

◎ Rather than asking the participants to tape their articles and photographs to the newsprint, do this exercise as a television newscast, allowing the young people each to read their articles or display their photographs.

NOTES

Use the space below to jot notes and reminders for the next time you use this strategy.

Resurrection Relay

A Bible Learning Activity for Easter

OVERVIEW

The point of this relay race is to quickly find passages on Easter themes in the four Gospels. The activity is intended to increase the young teens' skill in using the Bible and to help them become familiar with Gospel passages that recount the Resurrection of Jesus.

Suggested Time

About 15 minutes for the relay race and closing prayer; preparation time is extra

Group Size

The ideal group size for this strategy is sixteen participants. The activity can be done with a larger or smaller number of young people, though it will get a little drawn out with more than twenty-eight or so. See the Alternative Approaches section near the end of this strategy for suggestions on accommodating different numbers of participants.

Materials Needed

- ☼ four pieces of newsprint or poster board
- ☼ markers

- ☼ masking tape
- ☼ four small bowls or paper bags
- ☼ sixteen plastic eggs, four each of four different colors
- ☼ four spoons
- ☼ sixteen pieces of construction paper, approximately 3-by-6 inches, four each of approximately the same four different colors as the plastic eggs
- ☼ sixteen 1-by-3-inch strips of paper
- ☼ four Bibles
- ☼ four pieces of notebook paper
- ☼ four pens or pencils
- ☼ prizes for the winning team (optional)

PROCEDURE

Preparation. Make four signs on newsprint or poster board, one for each of the Gospels. Post the signs at one end of the meeting room. Place a Bible, a sheet of notebook paper, and a pen or pencil under each sign.

Prepare citation and question slips for each of the four Gospels. To avoid confusion you may want to work on one Gospel at a time. For each Gospel do the following things:

◎ Write each of the four citations listed below on a small slip of paper. Place each paper in a different colored egg. Put the four eggs and a spoon in a bowl or paper bag at the end of the room opposite the sign identifying the Gospel.

◎ Write the question associated with each citation on a piece of construction paper that is approximately the same color as the egg that contains the citation. Place the four questions facedown near the Bible.

The citations and their corresponding questions are as follows:

Citations	*Questions*
Matt. 28:1	With whom did Mary Magdalene go to inspect the tomb?
Matt. 28:7	Who were the women supposed to tell that Jesus had risen?
Matt. 28:13	What did the chief priests bribe the soldiers to do?
Matt. 28:19	What did Jesus tell the Apostles to do to all the nations?
Mark 16:1	Why did the women take perfumed oils to the tomb?
Mark 16:5	Whom did the women see when they entered the tomb?
Mark 16:9	To whom did the risen Jesus first appear?
Mark 16:19	Where is Jesus' seat in heaven?
Luke 24:2	What did the women find when they went to the tomb?
Luke 24:13	Where were the two disciples going?
Luke 24:30–31	When did the two disciples recognize Jesus?
Luke 24:39	What did Jesus show the Apostles in order to prove his identity?

John 20:13	Why was Mary Magdalene weeping?
John 20:15–16	When did Mary recognize Jesus?
John 20:25	What would have to happen for Thomas to believe that Jesus was alive?
John 20:29	Whom did Jesus bless?

1. Point out the signs identifying the four Gospels, and the bowls or bags of eggs. Divide the participants into four teams, one for each Gospel, and direct the teams each to line up behind a bowl or bag of eggs. Ask the first person in line from each team to go to the team's finish line at the opposite end of the room, under the sign that identifies the team's Gospel. That person is the team's Bible scholar.

2. Explain the following process in your own words:

The first person in the line picks an egg out of the bowl or bag, places it in the spoon, and runs to the team's Bible scholar at the other end of the room. If the egg falls out of the spoon, the runner must go back to the starting line and run again.

Once the runner reaches the team's Bible scholar, he or she picks up the question slip that matches the egg in color, and opens the egg and removes the citation inside it. The runner and the Bible scholar read the question, and look up the citation to find its answer. The runner writes the answer to the question on the notebook paper, then closes the Bible.

The runner now becomes the Bible scholar, and the former Bible scholar takes the spoon, runs back to the team, gives the spoon to the next person in line, and runs to the back of the line. The person who now has the spoon chooses an egg and repeats the procedure.

The game continues in this manner until all the teams' questions are answered. The team that finishes first and finds all the correct answers wins the game.

3. Facilitate the game. At the end, if you wish to, award the winners each a simple prize, such as a bookmark, a holy card, or a piece of Easter candy.

4. Gather the young people and lead them in the following litany:

Leader. On the third day, they went to Jesus' tomb and did not find him there. We respond . . .
All. Alleluia! He is risen, alleluia!

Leader. We thank you, Jesus, for dying for our sins. We respond . . .
All. Alleluia! He is risen, alleluia!

Leader. His friends saw him but at first did not recognize him. We respond . . .

All. Alleluia! He is risen, alleluia!

Leader. We have not seen and yet we believe and respond . . .

All. Alleluia! He is risen, alleluia!

Leader. Thank you, God, for giving us the Gospels. They are faithful reminders that death is not the end and that your promise of eternal life has been fulfilled. And so we respond . . .

All. Alleluia! He is risen, alleluia!

ALTERNATIVE APPROACHES

- If you have fewer than ten participants, create just two teams and give each team two sets of eggs and questions. If you have more than sixteen people in your group, find more Easter passages for each team, and write additional questions, so that each team member gets at least one citation and question.
- To make the game a little more challenging, mix up the passages among the teams so that no team is dealing with only one Gospel. Be sure to match the questions and citations for each team.
- If the game goes quickly and the young people are eager to try again, assign each team to a different Gospel.
- Invite the young people to make a bookmark of their favorite Resurrection passage: Give each person a lengthwise half of an index card. Make available a variety of decorating supplies. Tell the participants to write their favorite Resurrection passage on the bookmark and decorate the bookmark.
- Instead of doing the activity as a relay race, simply do it as a team competition. Give every young person on each team a Bible and designate a team captain. Ask one of the questions, announce its corresponding Bible passage, and tell the teams to look up the citation and find an answer. Follow these rules:
  - Only the team captain can answer the question for the team.
  - The first team to give the correct answer gets a point.
  - The game continues for no more than 15 minutes or until all the questions have been answered.
- This relay is not restricted to Easter passages. It can be used with other passages any time you want to give young teens a fun experience with searching the Scriptures.

NOTES

Use the space below to jot notes and reminders for the next time you use this strategy.

Be a Fool for Christ

A Prayer Service for April Fools' Day

This prayer service helps the young teens understand that being a fool can sometimes be admirable. It shows them that though some people might consider living by the teachings of Jesus to be foolish, Christians often have to do what is not popular in order to be true disciples.

Suggested Time

15 to 20 minutes

Group Size

This strategy can be done with any size group. If yours is larger than twenty people, you may want to recruit other adults to help with the prayer service so that you can have more than one line going at the same time in step 4.

Materials Needed

- ☼ newsprint and markers
- ☼ masking tape
- ☼ 3-by-5-inch index cards, one for each person
- ☼ pens or pencils

☼ a tape or CD player, and a recording of reflective music (optional)
☼ heart stickers, one for each person
☼ a basket

PROCEDURE

Preparation. Label the top of a sheet of newsprint "Foolish acts." Under that headline list the following ways of being a disciple. At the bottom of the sheet, leave space for writing other ways that the young people suggest. Post the list, but keep it covered until you are ready to use it.

◎ eating lunch with the most unpopular person in your class
◎ standing up to negative peer pressure
◎ praying before a meal in a restaurant
◎ standing up for someone whom others are putting down
◎ publicly taking a moral stance on an issue like sexual activity or alcohol consumption
◎ choosing not to cheat even if your grade depends on it
◎ telling the truth even if it gets you into trouble
◎ choosing to attend Mass instead of sleeping in

1. Direct the young people to arrange themselves in a circle, facing out. Tell them that you will read a series of statements. They are to listen carefully and follow your directions. Then read the following statements. After each statement wait until the young people are finished moving and then announce, "You are a fool for Christ!" Then ask for volunteers to share and explain their action. If no one steps forward when you read a statement, go on to the next statement.

If you have ever stood up for an underdog or someone who was picked on, take two steps forward.

If you have ever refused to do something other people were pressuring you to do, take two steps forward.

If you have ever decided to wear what you wanted and not what your peers said was okay, take one step forward.

If you have ever prayed publicly or discussed your faith with friends outside of church or religion class, take two steps forward.

If you have ever told the truth even though you knew it would get you in trouble, take two steps forward.

2. Gather the participants in front of the newsprint list you have posted and reveal its contents. Congratulate them for being fools for Christ, as evidenced by their movement in the previous step.

Point out that each statement on the posted list is a way that people their age can act as disciples, even when others may think that they are fools. Ask the young people to add other statements or decisions that might identify them as fools for Christ. List their ideas on the newsprint.

3. Give each participant an index card and a pen or pencil. Invite the young people each to choose one "foolish act" they will pledge to try, and to write it on their index card. Note that they may select an act from the list or write something that is not on the list.

4. Tell the young people that you will invite them to come forward one by one, bringing their index card with them. You will ask each person, "Are you a fool for Christ?" He or she is to respond: "Yes, I am. I have the courage to _____," naming in a few words the foolish act he or she wrote. Assure the participants that they do not have to divulge any personal information.

If you choose to play reflective music, start it at this point. Call the young people forward and follow the process you just described. When each person has answered, put a heart sticker on her or his cheek and say, "Go and be a disciple, for disciples are considered fools for Christ!" Provide a basket and tell the participants to place their card in it as they return to their place.

5. When everyone has placed their card in the basket, hold up the basket and say the following prayer or a spontaneous one on the same theme:

O God, we follow Jesus, and people call us fools. We turn to you for support and guidance, and remember that we are never alone in taking a stand for what is good. Bless us in the name of Jesus, your Son. Amen.

ALTERNATIVE APPROACHES

◎ Rather than presenting a ready-made list of foolish acts to the young people, have them brainstorm all the foolish acts they can think of, based on the opening experience for this strategy and on what they see among their friends and family. List those acts on newsprint as they are offered.

◎ If you have time, discuss with the group how easy or hard it is to do the foolish acts on the list, and the difficulties young people face in being a disciple. Ask the participants to describe moral dilemmas in their everyday life. Invite them to role-play some of the situations they describe. Discuss alternative solutions to the dilemmas.

SCRIPTURAL CONNECTIONS

- Matt. 5:1–12 (Blessed are they, for God's Reign is theirs.)
- Mark 6:2–4 (A prophet is not recognized among his or her own people.)
- John 15:18–19 (The world will hate you for following me.)
- 1 Cor. 3:18–19 (Those who wish to become wise must become fools.)

NOTES

Use the space below to jot notes and reminders for the next time you use this strategy.

Mary, Full of Grace

A Learning Activity for the Month of May

May is a month traditionally set aside to honor Mary the mother of Jesus. In this activity the young people hear about Mary and the church's devotion to her, make simple rosaries, and learn about the tradition of votive candles.

Suggested Time

35 to 45 minutes, depending on the size of the group

Group Size

This strategy works with any size group. However, if your group is larger than ten people, you may want to recruit other adults to help.

Materials Needed

- ☼ a pillar candle and matches
- ☼ a statue of Mary
- ☼ a Bible
- ☼ a table

☼ a variety of common household, outdoor, and office objects (such as a paper clip, safety pin, photograph, rock, bottle cap, battery, spoon, eraser, audiotape, piece of clay, small flower, button, cellophane tape, and rubber band), at least one for each person

☼ a rosary

☼ string or elastic, enough for each person to make a bracelet from it

☼ colored beads that can be strung on the string or elastic, twenty of one color and one of a second color for each person

☼ newsprint and markers

☼ masking tape

☼ votive candles or tea lights, one for each person

☼ a tape or CD player, and a recording of reflective music or a song honoring Mary (optional)

PROCEDURE

Preparation. Set up a prayer space with a pillar candle, a statue of Mary, a Bible, and votive candles or tea lights. On a table near the prayer space, display a collection of common household, outdoor, and office objects.

Print the words to the Hail Mary and the Lord's Prayer on newsprint. Post both prayers in a place where everyone can see them.

1. Gather the young people in the prayer space and light a pillar candle. Prayerfully raise up a statue of Mary and say, "Holy Mary, mother of God, pray for us."

Read Luke 1:46–49. Then present the following information in your own words:

The name the church has given to this passage is the Magnificat, from a Latin word that means "to magnify." The first line of the passage in some translations of the Bible is "My soul magnifies the Lord."

The Catholic church honors Mary in a special way because she said yes to God and because her body housed Jesus, the Son of God, from conception to birth. She tenderly mothered Jesus from infancy to adulthood, and continued to serve God by being with her Son until his death, and even beyond. Mary was one of Jesus' first disciples. She helped spread the word about his mission and message.

Note the difference between worshiping God and honoring Mary. We worship God and Jesus because they are divine. Mary was simply human, just like us. We honor her but do not worship her. This is a teaching that is sometimes misunderstood by Christians who are not Catholic.

2. Call the group's attention to the table of common objects you have arranged. Ask the participants to consider which object they would choose as an icon of Mary. You may need to define the word *icon* as "an object that in some way reminds us of God or a holy person." For example, a rock could be an icon of Mary because it reminds us that Mary's faith was as strong as a rock.

Direct the young people to choose their icon and return to their place. When everyone has made their selection, ask each person to explain how their icon reminds them of Mary.

3. Show the young people a rosary and explain that many people pray the rosary as a special devotion to Mary. Explain that the rosary is simply a collection of beads that are used to count prayers while meditating on events in the lives of Jesus and Mary.

Give each person a piece of string or elastic, long enough to tie around their wrist loosely. Also give each person twenty beads of one color and one bead of a second color. Tell the participants that they are each going to make a simplified rosary. Direct them to put ten beads of one color on their string or elastic, then the one bead of a different color, then the remaining ten beads of the first color. Have them tie their finished bracelets on one another's wrists, leaving enough room to slip the bracelets off easily.

4. Compare the full rosary with the ones the young people have made, and explain that the participants' bracelets are simplified rosaries. That is, they include just two decades, whereas the traditional rosary has five plus an opening sequence.

5. Display the prayers that you posted on newsprint. The young people are likely to know the Lord's Prayer, but many may not know the Hail Mary. If that is the case, explain that the Hail Mary begins with the words spoken by the angel Gabriel when he announced that Mary would bear God's Son (Luke 1:26–35). It also includes Elizabeth's words when Mary went to visit her (Luke 1:41–42).

Using the beads on the bracelets as counters, together pray the Hail Mary ten times, the Lord's Prayer once, and then the Hail Mary ten more times.

6. Explain that often in Catholic churches, votive candles are placed around a statue or painting of Mary. People light votive candles and pray for special needs. The tradition is that Mary hears those prayers and intercedes, or asks God to pay special attention to the needs of the people praying.

Invite the participants to go to the prayer space and each light a votive candle or tea light for a special need for themselves or for the world.

7. Close the session by asking the young people to sit quietly for a minute or two, reflecting on the votive candles. You may want to play reflective music or a song honoring Mary during this time. Invite the young people to pray their rosary silently if they wish.

Tell the participants to take their rosary home and use it as a private devotion anytime during the day or night.

ALTERNATIVE APPROACHES

◎ If you have extra time, begin the session by asking the young people what they know about Mary and the church's devotion to her. Let them tell the group what they already know. Fill in as many of the missing pieces as time allows.

◎ Though it will take a little more time, consider asking the young people to make an entire rosary. Several organizations provide inexpensive supplies for rosary making. They offer a kit that includes beads, wire, a small cross, and a medal. They also supply an instruction booklet for the mysteries of the rosary. One such group is Our Lady's Rosary Makers, P.O. Box 37080, Louisville, Kentucky 40233; phone 502-968-1434.

◎ Ask the young people to borrow a variety of Mary statues or portraits from relatives or elders in the parish. You might also put an ad in the parish bulletin, asking people to lend your group such items. Display these statues or portraits for the participants to examine, and perhaps invite the young people to compare and contrast the different representations.

◎ If people in your parish gather to pray the rosary before liturgy, suggest that the young people participate in the prayer.

◎ Invite a parish elder to tell the group about the tradition of May crownings.

SCRIPTURAL CONNECTIONS

◎ Luke 1:26–28 (The Annunciation occurs.)
◎ Luke 1:39–40 (Elizabeth honors Mary.)
◎ John 2:1–12 (Jesus and Mary attend the wedding at Cana.)
◎ Acts 1:14 (Mary prays with the disciples.)

NOTES

Use the space below to jot notes and reminders for the next time you use this strategy.

The Spirit Blows
A Hands-on Activity for Pentecost

OVERVIEW

At the beginning of this activity, the young people listen to a passage from the Acts of the Apostles that describes the coming of the Spirit as a strong, driving wind. They also discuss talents they can use in service to others. Finally they make a banner to sum up the activity and as a reminder that all gifts come from God and are to be used for the good of others.

Suggested Time

30 to 45 minutes, depending on the size of your group

Group Size

The ideal size group for this activity is eight to ten people, but a larger group works if you have enough adult support.

Materials Needed

- ☼ a candle and matches
- ☼ newsprint and markers
- ☼ a Bible
- ☼ 8-by-24-inch strips of red or white cloth, one for each person

☀ black or red permanent markers, one for each person

☀ items the participants can use as templates to trace a circle about 2 inches in diameter, such as small glasses, cardboard circles, or rolls of tape

☀ scissors that will cut cloth, one for each person

☀ wire hangers or dowels, approximately 12 inches long, one for each person

☀ double-sided tape or craft glue

PROCEDURE

Preparation. On a sheet of newsprint, write the following phrases: "The Spirit blows! We are never alone. We are called to share."

1. Gather the group and light a candle. While doing so comment to the young people that we use a candle to represent the light of Christ. It shines to remind us that God is always with us. Tell them that the candle will burn throughout the activity so that they remember that God is present. Then make the following comments in your own words:

The followers of Jesus had trouble believing that God was with them after Jesus died. In fact, the Apostles were so afraid that they hid. They were terrified that they would be arrested by the Roman authorities and abandoned by other followers of Jesus.

Followers of Jesus today know they are not alone and that God is always with them. Jesus taught that we have each been given a talent to use in service to others. When we use our gifts to help others, they feel supported and feel more closely connected with our school or parish community. They are not alone.

2. Brainstorm with the participants to identify the talents of people their age that can be used in service to the community. List all their ideas on newsprint in the form of personal qualities. The list might include good at listening, kind, helpful as a math tutor, playful with children, blessed with a good sense of humor, hardworking, a peacemaker, and so on.

3. Read Acts 2:1–4. Note that after the feast of Pentecost, the disciples began to teach and preach and follow the teachings of Jesus. Their courage came from their knowledge that they were not alone and that the Spirit of God was with them. The disciples also helped one another in a variety of ways. Each used his or her special talents to help the new community to survive and flourish.

4. Tell the participants that they will each make a wind banner as a reminder that they are never alone and that they are to use their talents for others. Guide the young people through the following process:

◎ Distribute strips of red or white cloth, markers (black if the material is red, or red if the material is white), circle templates, and scissors. Tell the young people to trace a circle in the center of their strip of cloth and carefully cut it out. Note that the hole will allow wind to blow through the banner rather than pulling it off the hanger or dowel they will attach it to.

◎ Point out the newsprint you posted before the session. Direct everyone to copy the words from it onto their banner using the markers you have distributed.

◎ Tell the young people that they are also to identify one or more talents that they possess that can be used in service to others. Point out the list of suggestions the group created, and explain that they may use talents from the list or others that they think of. Instruct them to write their talents on the banner. As they write each gift, they should think of specific situations in which it is necessary.

◎ Invite the young people to sign their name on everyone else's banners. Remind them that much like the disciples after Jesus died, they make up a small Christian community within their parish community and within the broader church.

◎ Affix each banner to a hanger or dowel by folding the top of the banner over the hanger or dowel and attaching it to itself with double-sided tape or craft glue.

5. Gather the young people and their banners and have everyone listen as you read Acts 2:42–47. Invite the young people each to hang their banner in their home or on a tree outside of their house to remind them that they are not alone and that the Spirit will guide them to use their talents in service to others.

ALTERNATIVE APPROACHES

◎ As the young people are working and you read the closing passage from Acts of the Apostles, have electric fans blowing around the room to give a sense of movement.

◎ If you have more time, provide additional supplies for decorating the banners. Encourage the young people to be creative and colorful.

◎ Hang all the banners in your meeting place for a week or two. Or arrange to hang the banners in a gathering space in the parish.

◎ Make the strips of cloth into wind socks instead of banners. Do this by rolling the strips lengthwise and stitching the sides together. Do not cut a hole for the wind; the cylinder will blow freely in the breeze. Punch two holes on opposite sides of one opening, tie one end of a string through those holes, and tie the other end of the string to a hanger or dowel. You may need to reinforce this attachment with superglue or duct tape.

◎ As a follow-up to this activity, the next time you gather with the young people, talk about ways they have used their gifts since they made their banners.

SCRIPTURAL CONNECTIONS

- Matt. 5:13–16 (You are salt of the earth, light of the world.)
- 1 Cor. 12:4–11 (There are many gifts from one Spirit.)
- James 1:17 (Every gift comes from God.)
- 1 Pet. 4:3–10 (Work together and share your gifts.)

NOTES

Use the space below to jot notes and reminders for the next time you use this strategy.

Tower of Independence

A Discussion Activity
for Independence Day

This activity uses the popular game Jenga to guide the young people in a discussion about healthy and unhealthy dependence and independence.

Suggested Time

25 to 35 minutes, or longer if the group is interested in continuing the game

Group Size

This strategy works well with eight or fewer people for each Jenga game. If you have more than eight young teens in your group, you need more than one game. It would also be a good idea to recruit other adults to help monitor the tower topics discussions if you use more than one game.

Special Considerations

If you have more than eight people in your group, you might want to put a note in the parish bulletin a few weeks before the event, asking to borrow Jenga games or other tumbling tower games.

Materials Needed

☼ Jenga games or other tumbling tower games, one for every eight people
☼ copies of resource 2, "Tower Topics," one for every Jenga game
☼ a scissors
☼ small U.S. flags, one for each person (optional)

PROCEDURE

Preparation. Stack each Jenga tower on a flat surface such as a hard floor, a small table, or a TV tray.

Make a copy of resource 2, "Tower Topics," for each Jenga game. Cut apart the questions as scored and place them in a stack near the game.

1. Open the session by explaining that the group will explore what it means to be independent and dependent. Read the following prayer or say a spontaneous prayer on the same theme:

O God, you want only what is best for us. Guide us as we grow toward being more independent of and interdependent with others, so that we recognize and accept that we are dependent on you. May we learn that to be free means that we must be responsible with our freedom. We ask this in the name of our great teacher, Jesus. Amen.

2. If some participants are not familiar with Jenga, point out the towers you have erected and explain that the object of the game is to take turns removing a block from the middle of the tower and putting it on top without toppling the tower. Note that in the version they will play today, before placing the block on the top of the tower, they must choose a question from a stack of tower topics and answer it.

When you are sure everyone understands the process, divide the participants into groups of about eight. Tell the groups each to begin their game with the person who was born closest to the Fourth of July. If someone knocks the tower down before everyone has a turn, restack the wooden blocks so that everyone else can have a turn. If everyone answers a question before the tower is knocked down, then allow the game to continue until the tower is down or all the questions have been answered.

3. After all the groups have finished their games, gather the young people in a circle. Make the following points in your own words:

No one is totally dependent or independent. People grow toward independence in some ways, and toward dependence in others.

It is important to grow in ways that allow us to be our best selves. That means becoming independent of those who call us to imitation or trendiness. It means gradually becoming financially independent from parents as we learn how to support ourselves. It means growing in our awareness of our dependence on God.

An important concept to understand is that of healthy *interdependence*. We will always need other people, and we will always be needed by others. That is part of who we are as community. One sign of maturity is recognizing our need for others and the contribution we make to the world.

4. If you have small flags available, give one to each person. Then read the following words of prayer:

> O God, we come before you aware that freedom includes responsibility. We now pray for the needs of our country: . . .

Invite the young people to raise up in prayer any current national issues. Then continue with the prayer:

> We also pray for the countries that struggle for independence from political groups and from things like fear, war, and starvation. . . .

Invite the young people to add prayers for the world, especially for other countries that are struggling for independence. Then continue as follows:

> We also pray for ourselves, that we might grow in our sense of independence from the ways of the world, healthy interdependence with other people, and dependence on God. . . .

Invite the participants to add prayers for people their age, especially those who struggle to find their place in the world. Then conclude the prayer as follows:

> We ask you, God, to bless each of us, our country, and the leaders of the world, and guide us all to do what is just and according to your will. Amen.

ALTERNATIVE APPROACHES

- Give each person a wooden block. Allow time for everyone to consider an area of independence with which they struggle. Invite them each to write on their block a word that suggests that issue. Give them the block to take home and use as a reminder to turn to God in prayer when that issue arises.
- After the game direct the young people to work in pairs to come up with additional questions that deal with independence. Invite them to play the game again with the new questions.
- This strategy is not limited to Independence Day. The Jenga tower game can be adapted as a discussion-starter for almost any situation.

SCRIPTURAL CONNECTIONS

- Ps. 118:5–9 (I trusted God, and God set me free.)
- Matt. 6:26–32 (God will provide all you need.)
- Phil. 4:19–20 (Praise God, who gives you what you need.)

NOTES

Use the space below to jot notes and reminders for the next time you use this strategy.

Tower Topics

What does the word *independence* mean to you?

What is one way you can become more independent of your friends?

Does being an adult mean being independent of everyone? Explain.

In what ways are you dependent on a friend? In what ways is your friend dependent on you?

What is one way you can become be more independent of your parents?

In what ways are you dependent on your community?

Who is the most independent person you know? Why did you pick that person?

Does your community depend on you for anything? Explain.

In what ways are you most dependent on your family?

In what ways are you independent of your community? Is your independence a good thing?

Why is independence important to countries around the world?

What is one aspect of your culture that you wish people your age could be independent from?

In what ways was Jesus dependent on others?

How does someone your age know that he or she is dependent on God?

What is one way people are dependent on God?

Why is it important for people to be independent of a government that is very strict and cruel?

What is one healthy way that someone your age is independent of other people?

What is one way you are dependent on the church?

How do you know when dependence on another person is unhealthy?

Who models for you what it means to grow in healthy dependent and independent ways?

What are some ways that people your age are dependent on their culture?

In what ways was Jesus independent of others?

TGIS
(Thank God It's Summer)!

An End-of-School Celebration

This celebration is intended simply to bring young teens together to have fun in a community of faith.

Suggested Time

90 to 120 minutes, depending on how long people stay at the various stations

Group Size

This strategy works well with more than eight and no more than thirty-two participants.

Special Considerations

Even if your group is small, it will be difficult to do this activity without help. The more adult aids you recruit, the more easily the activities will flow from one to another. Divide the adults into teams to supervise the various activities. High school youth can help direct the activities, but they should always be teamed with an adult.

Because this strategy is messy, it is best held outdoors.

Materials Needed

- a Bible
- a small wading pool
- water toys such as cups, pitchers, spray bottles, little boats, and rubber ducks
- a garden hose
- a garden sprinkler
- a volleyball net
- two bedsheets
- two laundry baskets
- fifteen to twenty filled water balloons
- a sandbox or a second wading pool, filled with sand
- sand toys such as pails, shovels, diggers, hand rakes, and miniature die-cast cars and construction equipment
- a picnic table or a long table
- 5-by-7-inch index cards or pieces of white poster board, one for each person
- a mixed collection of seashells, rocks, leaves, twigs, flowers, or other natural elements, eight to ten items for each person
- glue
- markers
- other items for making and decorating posters (optional)
- a coach's whistle or a handbell
- snacks and refreshments

PROCEDURE

Preparation. Look over the materials needed checklist. Borrow from parish members items that you do not have.

Notify the participants at least a week before the event. Let them know the details of the event and encourage them to bring or wear clothing that they do not mind getting wet.

On the day of the event, set up the following stations:

- *Water play.* a small wading pool filled with water and water toys, and a garden hose and sprinkler hooked up to a water supply
- *Water balloon volleyball.* a volleyball net, and on each side of the net, a bedsheet and a laundry basket containing water balloons
- *Sandbox buddies.* a sand box or small wading pool filled with sand and sand toys

◎ *Praise posters.* a picnic table or long table, with index cards or pieces of poster board, small nature elements, glue, markers, and other poster-making supplies if you have them

1. When the participants arrive, gather them in one place and announce that they will be celebrating the end of school and arrival of summer. Invite one of the young people or an adult leader to read Psalm 100. Conclude with the following prayer:

O God, we come today to praise you in joy-filled fun. Thank you for summer and a break from studies. May we play and pray with joy today because all you have created is very, very good. We ask this in the name of Jesus, who lives and reigns with you, and the Holy Spirit, one God, forever and ever. Amen.

2. Direct the participants to form small groups by counting off by four and joining those who call out the same number. Assign each small group to one of the four activity stations you prepared earlier. Explain that when the groups hear a whistle or bell, they are to move to the next activity. Rotate the groups through the activities every 15 to 30 minutes, depending on how much time you have, until all the groups have enjoyed all the activities.

Direct the activities at the stations as follows:

◎ *Water play.* Invite the young people to wade and splash in the pool, play with the water toys, and run through the hose and sprinkler.

◎ *Water balloon volleyball.* Divide the group into two teams. Direct the teams to go to opposite sides of the volleyball net and hold their bedsheet by its corners and sides. Place a water balloon in the middle of one team's sheet. Explain that the object of the game is to toss the water balloon over the net to the other team, which must catch it in its sheet. When the balloon breaks, the throwing team gets a point and another water balloon to toss. If the receiving team catches the balloon unbroken, the volleying continues until the balloon breaks. Present this clue: The higher the balloon is tossed, the more likely it is to break on impact.

◎ *Sandbox buddies.* Instruct the group members to work together to build sand castles and sculptures, or to build roads and play with small cars and trucks.

◎ *Praise posters.* Give each person an index card or piece of poster board, glue, markers, and eight to ten seashells, pebbles, leaves, or whatever you have gathered from nature. Tell the young people to arrange the natural materials into a design or pattern and glue them onto the poster board. Invite them to use markers to decorate their collage and to write on it the words, "All creation, praise God!" If you have supplied other decorating materials, encourage the participants to use them creatively.

3. After everyone has circulated through all four stations, stop the play. Gather the young people in a circle and ask them to share their praise posters while you read Psalm 150. Conclude with snacks and refreshments.

ALTERNATIVE APPROACHES

◎ Instead of forming small groups by having the young people count off, use a creative grouper such as those that follow. Other ideas are presented in many youth ministry books, including *Community-Building Ideas for Ministry with Young Teens* in this series.

  ◎ Form groups according to the season of the year in which people were born.

  ◎ Arrange for adult leaders to paint the young people's faces as they arrive. Use four different images for the paintings, and group the young teens according to the image on their faces. You might want to appoint one adult leader to keep track of how many young people receive each painting, to ensure that the groups come out even.

  ◎ Give each person a playing card when he or she arrives, being sure that cards of the four suits are distributed evenly among the participants. Group the young people according to suits.

  ◎ Cut the front panels of greeting cards or cereal boxes into four puzzle pieces. Distribute the pieces. Then direct the young people to find the other people who have pieces that match.

◎ Young people love to invite their friends to their fun activities. Tell the participants that they may each ask a friend to attend this event. Arrange for extra adults; if the numbers exceed thirty-two, set up additional or duplicate stations.

◎ If you have more than thirty-two participants, if you want more stations so that you can expand the event, or if the stations described in the Procedure section will not appeal to your young teens, set up other stations. Here are some ideas:

  ◎ an obstacle course

  ◎ tricycle races

  ◎ a kite-flying area

  ◎ an Ultimate Frisbee contest

  ◎ an ice-blocking hill (For this activity purchase one 10- or 25-pound block of ice for every two or three people, place the blocks at the top of a grassy hill, and put a folded towel on top of each. Instruct the participants to sit on a block of ice and slide down the hill. You may encourage races, trains, and slaloms to vary the fun. Depending on how hot it is, a single 10-pound block of ice lasts about an hour and a half.)

◎ This strategy can easily become a family event. Recruit a team of volunteers and design the events so that they involve families as team members. For example, the water balloon volleyball teams would be made up of the young people in your group and their parents and siblings.

NOTES

Use the space below to jot notes and reminders for the next time you use this strategy.

Back-to-School Blessing
A Prayer Service for the Beginning of the School Year

OVERVIEW

This blessing ceremony celebrates the beginning of school and helps the young people welcome a new school year. It is ideal to use for the first meeting of a group in a new school year.

Suggested Time

10 to 20 minutes, depending on the size of the group

Group Size

The ideal size for this activity is a group of ten to thirty.

Special Considerations

Some of the young people in your group may be starting in a new school this year. As with any change in life, they may experience a wide variety of feelings, such as excitement, nervousness, and fear. Be sure to pay attention to their anxieties and help them to focus on the positive aspects of a new school and school year.

Materials Needed

- ☼ a backpack
- ☼ items that represent mind learning, such as school supplies, textbooks, a calculator, a globe, and musical instruments
- ☼ items that represent body learning, such as sports equipment, dance or gymnastics supplies, and physical education attire
- ☼ items that represent spirit learning, such as a book of prayers, a religious symbol or icon, a flower, a flyer for a service project, and a journal
- ☼ a pillar candle and matches
- ☼ a Bible
- ☼ a clear bowl of water
- ☼ a small branch from an evergreen tree
- ☼ new pens or pencils, one for each person

PROCEDURE

Preparation. Before the young people arrive, establish a prayer space with a backpack; items that represent mind-learning, body learning, and spirit learning; a pillar candle; a Bible; a clear bowl of water; a small branch from an evergreen tree; and a new pen or pencil for each person.

1. Gather the young people in the prayer space. Make a comment about the gift of new beginnings as the school year opens. Acknowledge the participants' anxieties, particularly if some of them are starting classes at a new school. Tell them that together they will begin a new school year with a blessing.

2. Invite the young people to observe in silence the items in the prayer space that can be considered tools for school. Point out that some of the items are for "mind learning"—things like textbooks, a calculator, a globe, and musical instruments. Other items are for "body learning"; sports equipment and dance supplies fall into this category. The last category is "spirit learning"; it includes items like a religious icon and a personal journal.

3. Light a pillar candle. Then read 1 Tim. 4:12–16. Return the Bible to the prayer space and pick up a bowl of water. Dip an evergreen branch in the bowl and sprinkle the items in the prayer space. As you do so, say the following prayer:

O God, we ask your blessing on these symbols of a new year. May they help us to learn, and to enjoy and to share the special talents that you have given to us. We ask this in the name of Jesus, who lives and reigns with you and the Holy Spirit, one God, forever and ever. Amen.

4. Ask the young people to move toward you one by one, with their hands in front of them, palms up. As each person reaches you, dip your thumb in the water and make the sign of the cross on her or his forehead, palms, shoulders, and feet as you say, "[Name of young person], use your mind and body this school year to learn, to serve, and to grow." Then give the person a pen or pencil before the person returns to her or his place.

5. To conclude the blessing service, make a few comments as follows, in your own words:

◎ Remind the young people that they represent the Christian community in their school, and that they should offer hospitality to others. Encourage them to look for and befriend younger and new students.

◎ Note how important it is for all young people to feel like they are wanted and that they belong to the school community. Challenge the participants to include all fellow students in social gatherings, reach out to people at lunchtime, and pay attention to people who seem to be alone a lot.

◎ Tell them that the beginning of a new school year means a chance to start anew. Challenge them to establish good study habits right from the start, especially if that has been a problem in previous years. Encourage them to work at staying focused so that they can succeed academically and know that they are doing their best.

ALTERNATIVE APPROACHES

◎ If you have extra time, allow the young people to express their feelings about beginning a new school year.

◎ Consider putting all the mind, body, and spirit items in the backpack when you set up the prayer space. In step 2 ask the young people to take turns removing one item at a time and explaining what it represents and how it can help a person develop brain learning, body learning, or spirit learning. Note that many of the items can address more than one type of learning.

NOTES

Use the space below to jot notes and reminders for the next time you use this strategy.

Fears

A Discussion Exercise
for Halloween

This combination name-tag game and small-group exercise is designed to uncover some fears of young adolescents. In addition to naming fears, the participants brainstorm ways to deal with them.

Suggested Time

20 to 30 minutes, or slightly longer with a large group

Group Size

This strategy can be done with any size group.

Materials Needed

- ☼ Halloween decorations
- ☼ light-colored construction paper, a half sheet for each person
- ☼ markers, one for each person
- ☼ newsprint
- ☼ masking tape
- ☼ a tape or CD player, and a recording of Halloween music or sounds

☼ sheets of paper and pens or pencils (or sheets of newsprint and markers), one for each small group

☼ a Bible

☼ a recording of a song that deals with our fears and God (optional)

PROCEDURE

Preparation. Before the young people arrive, decorate the meeting space in a Halloween motif and make the room as dark as possible. List the following items on newsprint. The examples in brackets are for your information only.

◎ favorite Halloween candy

◎ favorite scary movie

◎ favorite Halloween game [e.g., bobbing for apples, or pin the hat on the witch]

◎ favorite Halloween character [e.g., black cat, witch, or ghost]

◎ favorite movie monster [e.g., Godzilla, King Kong, or Frankenstein]

1. After everyone has gathered, turn up the lights and give each person a half sheet of construction paper and a marker. Point out the list of favorites you have posted. Tell everyone to write their name and their own favorites on their paper. When they are finished, they should tape the paper to the front of their clothing.

2. Announce that the participants are each to find three other people who have at least one of the same favorites as they listed. When they have found those three people, they are to sit down together.

While the young people are moving around, play a recording of Halloween music or sounds.

3. Tell the participants to figure out who in their group has the birthday closest to Halloween. Explain that beginning with that person and moving to his or her left, the group members are each to name two things they were afraid of when they were young children. Allow about a minute and a half for each group to complete this task.

4. Give one person in each group a piece of paper and a pen or pencil, or a sheet of newsprint and a marker. Explain that each group is to name three things that middle school or junior high students are generally afraid of—for example, a completely dark room at bedtime. The person who has the paper should write down the ideas, leaving space after each one. Allow 2 or 3 minutes for this task.

After the groups have brainstormed the fears of young teens, tell them to list some things that can be done about each fear. For example, if the fear is of a completely dark room, they might use a night-light or place a flashlight near the bed. Allow 2 or 3 minutes for this task.

5. Call the groups together. List on newsprint the fears and solutions they came up with. Or, if the groups already wrote their ideas on newsprint, have them post the sheets, and then review the sheets.

Tell the young people that all people—even adults—experience fears of some kind. When we figure out ways to cope with our fears, we seem to feel a little less afraid. Other people in our life can help us find solutions that make us feel more at peace.

6. Read Isa. 41:10. Then say the following prayer or one that you create spontaneously on the same theme:

> O God, help us to turn to you when we are afraid. We trust your promise that you will always be with us. We ask this in the name of Jesus.

You may want to conclude with a recording of a hymn that deals with fear and God.

ALTERNATIVE APPROACHES

◎ Though Halloween is the ideal time for this activity, fear is a year-round issue. This strategy can be used any time of year, with or without the Halloween decorations and recording.

◎ Using the passages listed in the following Scriptural Connections section, ask the young people to work with their small group to sum up in ten words or less what God says about handling fear. If time allows, you might encourage them to create a poster or a T-shirt of their summary statement.

◎ For the closing prayer, ask one or more of the participants to choose and read a prayer about fear from *Prayers Before an Awesome God: The Psalms for Teenagers,* by David Haas (Winona, MN: Saint Mary's Press, 1998), or *Looking Past the Sky: Prayers by Young Teens,* edited by Marilyn Kielbasa (Winona, MN: Saint Mary's Press, 1999).

◎ Follow this Halloween activity by asking the young people to trick-or-treat in the neighborhood for charity. They might collect money for relief efforts or nonperishable goods for the local food shelf. Announce the collection at the parish or in local media for a few weeks before Halloween. Be sure to provide the trick-or-treaters with a note explaining the activity, in case people want to check its legitimacy. Also invite other adults to participate so that the young people have adequate supervision.

SCRIPTURAL CONNECTIONS

- Ps. 56:4 (When we are afraid, we can turn to God.)
- Isa. 41:10 (God is always with us.)
- Isa. 44:8 (God has chosen us as witnesses.)
- Matt. 6:25–34 (Do not worry about tomorrow.)
- Luke 12:32–34 (God takes care of us.)

NOTES

Use the space below to jot notes and reminders for the next time you use this strategy.

Trick-or-Treat for a Cause

An Outreach Activity for Halloween

OVERVIEW | This strategy is a twist on the traditional Halloween practice of going door to door for treats, which many young teens consider childish but at the same time are reluctant to give up. Instead of collecting candy, the trick-or-treaters gather food and donations for a local food pantry.

Suggested Time

About 60 minutes for the planning meeting, plus an evening for the trick-or-treating

Group Size

This strategy works best with a group of fifteen or fewer young teens, but it can work with more people, as long as you have enough adult support.

Special Considerations

It is important to get out the word that the young teens will be collecting food and donations, so that people in the collection area will be informed and expecting their visit. Also be sure to arrange enough adult supervision to ensure the safety of the young people as well as to provide transportation.

Materials Needed

- ☼ a map of the area to be covered (optional)
- ☼ several sheets of poster board, markers, and other supplies for making posters
- ☼ writing supplies for newspaper and bulletin articles
- ☼ index cards, one for each person
- ☼ several cardboard boxes for hauling the collected food
- ☼ snacks and refreshments

PROCEDURE

Preparation. Recruit adults to help out as drivers, chaperones, and aids.

Planning Meeting

1. About a month before Halloween, gather the young people for a planning meeting and introduce the idea of trick-or-treating to help people who are poor. You might start by telling the participants that Halloween began as a celebration of the vigil before All Saints' Day. Note that *hallow* means "holy" or "sacred," and *een* is a short version of the word *evening.* Tell the young teens that by trick-or-treating for those who are poor, they will be doing holy work, in keeping with the original intention of the holiday.

2. Guide the young people in the following tasks:

- ◎ Decide on the area to be covered by the trick-or-treaters. Use a map of the neighborhood, if you have one. Also decide how the young people will be divided into small groups, what each group's territory will be, and which adult will go along with each group to drive and collect food.
- ◎ Make posters alerting people in the neighborhood to the project. The posters should include the following information:
  - ◎ the date and time that the trick-or-treaters will be in the neighborhood
  - ◎ the types of items you will be collecting, including a request for cash donations to purchase perishable items
  - ◎ a note that the trick-or-treaters will be carrying special identification
- ◎ Recruit adults and young teens to take the posters to area businesses for display and to hang them in public places as well as around the parish. (This task can be completed after the planning meeting if necessary.)
- ◎ Decide whether people should come in costume.
- ◎ Write an article for the local newspaper and another for the parish bulletin, with the same information that is on the posters.

Trick-or-Treating

Preparation. For each participant make up an index card that identifies her or him as a trick-or-treater from your parish. Be sure the young person's name is on the card, or leave space to write it later. Put a note on the card, stating who checks should be made out to, in case someone wants to donate money.

1. On the evening of the collection, gather with the young people and the drivers. Distribute the cards that you have made, identifying the trick-or-treaters as being from the parish. Discuss with the participants what to say when someone comes to the door, and how to identify themselves and their project.

Say a prayer of blessing on them and on those who will benefit from their work. Send them off with instructions to return by a given time.

2. When the young people return, help them organize the food into cardboard boxes. Provide snacks and refreshments.

3. At the first opportunity, take the food and donations to the local food pantry. You may want to invite a few young people to go along so that they can see where some of the work of helping poor people is done.

ALTERNATIVE APPROACHES

◎ Arrange for the young people to collect (instead of food) mittens, hats, scarves, blankets, sweatshirts, and any other items that would be useful to poor families in the coming winter.

◎ As part of the planning evening, invite the young teens to make T-shirts identifying themselves as being with your parish. You can purchase inexpensive white T-shirts at discount or odd-lots stores. Permanent markers or fabric paints can be used to create brightly colored designs on the shirts.

◎ In addition to canvassing the neighborhood on Halloween itself, set up a food collection point at the parish on the weekend before Halloween and ask people to bring in nonperishable items or cash donations.

◎ In addition to organizing the trick-or-treating event for young teens, invite the younger children of the parish to drop off some of their wrapped Halloween candy after their own traditional trick-or-treating. Package the candy in sandwich bags, and give the bags to the local food pantry for distribution along with the food collected by the young teens.

◎ When the young people return from their routes, have a surprise Halloween party waiting for them. Ask parents or high school youth to come in and decorate the meeting place and set up the food and beverages. The volunteers could also lead the group in Halloween games and in the singing of pumpkin carols (Christmas carols with the words changed). *Holiday Ideas for*

Youth Groups (by Wayne Rice and Mike Yaconelli, 1981), part of the Ideas Library series, is a useful resource for such an event. The series is published by Youth Specialties. Check the company's web site, *www.youthspecialties.com,* or call the company at 800-776-8008.

NOTES

Use the space below to jot notes and reminders for the next time you use this strategy.

Unmasking Saints
A Learning Activity
for All Saints' Day

This creative activity helps young adolescents learn a little about their Catholic heritage by exploring the life and work of their patron saint or a favorite saint.

Suggested Time

45 to 60 minutes, depending on how elaborate the projects are

Group Size

This strategy works best with no more than ten young people.

Materials Needed

- ☼ biographical books about saints
- ☼ access to the Internet (optional)
- ☼ pieces of white poster board, 10-by-14 inches, one for each person
- ☼ scissors
- ☼ markers
- ☼ pencils
- ☼ yarn
- ☼ colored paper

- ☀ scraps of material
- ☀ glue
- ☀ a hole punch
- ☀ string
- ☀ newsprint

PROCEDURE

Preparation. Before meeting with your group, reflect on the story of your own patron saint or a saint that you admire.

Write the following sentence-starters on newsprint:

- ◎ My saint's name is . . .
- ◎ My saint lived . . . (when and where)
- ◎ Something interesting I found out about my saint is . . .

1. Introduce the activity by briefly making, in your own words, the following comments on the significance of saints in our heritage:

Saints are people like us who had a deep relationship with God. Their lives are inspirational, and they can serve as holy mentors for our own faith journeys.

Patron saints are either saints whose name we share or saints who have a connection to our work or hobby.

2. Make available to the young people a variety of biographical books about saints. Tell them to look up their patron saint or a favorite saint. If someone has a name that is common to several saints, tell them to read various biographies and choose the saint that they would like to hold up as a model. For example, someone with the name John could choose Saint John the Baptist, Saint John the Evangelist, Saint John of the Cross, Saint John Baptist de La Salle, or another Saint John.

Ask the young people to work in teams and to share the resources if necessary. If access to the Internet is available, allow some young teens to work on the computer. One web site that contains information on all known saints is *http://saints.catholic.org.*

3. Give each young person a 10-by-14-inch piece of white poster board. Provide a variety of tools, including scissors, markers, pencils, yarn, colored paper, scraps of material, and glue. Tell the participants to make a mask of what they imagine their saint looked like, striving to be as authentic as possible. For example, if their patron saint is female, was she a nun? a child? a young woman? Note that the mask should look like the real person in her or his time, not like a cartoon character or an abstract person. Set a clear time limit for this part of the activity.

When the young people have each finished their mask, tell them to punch a hole on either side of it and attach string so that they can tie it around their head.

4. After everyone has finished, invite them to put on their mask. Then display the newsprint list of sentence-starters you have prepared, and ask the young people to complete the sentences aloud.

5. To conclude this exercise, ask everyone, with their mask on, to stand in a circle. Invite each person to state loudly the name of her or his saint. Pray the following prayer, or a spontaneous prayer on the same theme:

O God, may we learn to follow your ways as these saints have done. Help us to become holy people who teach others how to grow closer to you. For all the saints we have named, and for those who are yet undiscovered, we are grateful. Amen.

ALTERNATIVE APPROACHES

- Begin the activity by asking the young people to come up with a definition of a saint. They might work in small groups to complete this sentence: "A saint is someone who . . ."
- Expand the discussion part of this activity by asking the young people for ideas about modern saints. For example, you might ask who they think young people fifty years from now will be reading about in a book about saints. Or ask them who in their daily life they consider to have saintly qualities.
- Explain to the group how someone becomes a saint. Your parish or local library should have a book on Catholic practices that provides information on canonization.

NOTES

Use the space below to jot notes and reminders for the next time you use this strategy.

Giving Thanks for Special People

A Communication Activity for Thanksgiving

OVERVIEW

This communication activity invites the young people to complete a sentence-starter as a quick and nonthreatening way to thank special people in their life. It is an ideal activity for Thanksgiving time because the participants are already focused on giving thanks.

Suggested Time

About 10 minutes

Group Size

This strategy can be done with any size group.

Materials Needed

- ☼ 3-by-5-inch index cards, one for each person
- ☼ pens or pencils, one for each person
- ☼ envelopes, one for each person
- ☼ newsprint and markers

☼ stickers, rubber stamps, colored pencils, and anything else that can be used for decorating a card (optional)

☼ first-class stamps, one for each person (optional)

PROCEDURE

Preparation. Before the young people arrive, write the following sentence-starter on newsprint: "I give God thanks for you. You are a special gift in my life, and I want to thank you for _____."

1. Explain to the young people that they are going to prepare a special thank-you card to someone who has helped them or has shown them care within the last month or so. Ask them to think about parents, teachers, coaches, Scout leaders, neighbors, relatives, youth leaders, and friends who have supported them in some way, and to identify one they would like to thank. If your group opens up easily, go around it and ask each participant to name the person or to simply describe the situation.

2. Give each person one 3-by-5-inch index card, a pen or pencil, and an envelope. Display the newsprint statement you created before the session. Tell the young people to copy the sentence from the newsprint onto their card, adding the reason they have chosen to thank the person who has helped them. Explain that they will be sending that person the card when they are done. If you have time and materials, allow them to decorate the card.

3. Direct the participants to write the name and address of the card's recipient on the envelope. You may need to provide a phone book so that the young people can look up addresses. They may either deliver the card in person or mail it.

ALTERNATIVE APPROACHES

◎ Though this activity is a natural for Thanksgiving, it can be done at any time of the year.

◎ Hold a Thanksgiving party and allow the young people to write and send as many thank-you cards as they want. Include time for them to decorate their cards with Thanksgiving motifs.

◎ Designate a monthly thank-you–card night, allowing 10 or 15 minutes for the young teens to write notes to anyone who has shown them care that month. Announce the activity before each gathering and tell the young people to bring the addresses of those they want to thank. You might also specify a category to focus on each month. For example, one month the young people could write notes to relatives, the next to teachers, the next to people their age whom they admire, the next to adults not related to them, and so forth.

◎ Instruct the young people to make and send bookmarks in addition to thank-you cards. Cut index cards in half lengthwise and provide materials for the participants each to create a bookmark for the person they are writing to. They might start with a scriptural verse, such as Phil. 1:3, "I thank my God every time I remember you."

SCRIPTURAL CONNECTIONS

◎ Prov. 15:30 (Recognition delights others.)
◎ Sir. 6:14–16 (A faithful friend is a treasure.)
◎ Phil. 1:3–6 (I thank my God for you.)

NOTES

Use the space below to jot notes and reminders for the next time you use this strategy.

Build a Meal

An Outreach Activity
for Thanksgiving

This outreach activity invites the young people to build holiday meals and memories for families that might not be able to afford a traditional Thanksgiving meal.

Suggested Time

10 to 15 minutes for the planning meeting to discuss the project; 20 to 30 minutes to assemble the meal, decorate a tablecloth, and write or find prayers

Group Size

This strategy can be done with any size group. The more people you have, the more meals they can build.

Materials Needed

- ☼ newsprint and markers
- ☼ boxes or baskets, one for each meal
- ☼ plain white paper tablecloths, one for each family that will receive a meal
- ☼ colored markers and other supplies for decorating the tablecloths
- ☼ supplies for making prayer cards (optional)

PROCEDURE

Preparation. Before the event identify families that can use the meals and also determine how many meals your group can make. Check with the pastoral staff in your parish. You may also contact the agent for social-justice outreach at your parish or the local welfare office, Salvation Army office, soup kitchen, or Catholic Charities office. Establish a delivery location for each meal.

Place an ad in the parish bulletin, asking for monetary donations. Those donations can be used to purchase perishable items at the last minute, to buy expensive items like turkeys, and so on. Be sure that you have enough refrigerator or freezer room to store the perishable goods for as long as you need to.

Planning Meeting

1. Explain to the young people that they are going to build a Thanksgiving meal for a special family. Each of them will bring some food item to put in a box or basket, and together they will work on other elements to make the meal memorable.

2. With the help of the young people, list on newsprint the food items that are part of a traditional Thanksgiving meal. Be sure the following items are on the list: a roasting chicken or turkey, stuffing, potatoes, gravy, cranberry sauce, a vegetable, bread or rolls, and a dessert.

3. Ask the young people to write their name beside the item they think they can bring to your next gathering. If you have more items than participants, some people may be able to bring two things. If you have more participants than items, you can build more than one meal.

Building the Meal

Preparation. You may want to call the young people or send them a reminder before this session, so that they do not forget to bring their item or items.

1. Set out a box or basket for each meal, and ask the young people to put their nonperishable food items in the container. Save room for the perishable foods, which will have to be refrigerated or frozen until the delivery date. If you are building more than one meal, be sure that the food items get into the correct box or basket.

2. Once the food items have been collected, ask the young teens to decorate a paper tablecloth for each family that will receive a meal. They might include good wishes for the family, a Thanksgiving greeting, verses from the Scriptures, and promises of prayer. They could write on the tablecloth a prayer to be read at the meal. They might also create for each family member a special prayer card with a blessing prayer. When they have finished the tablecloth and prayer cards, add them to the box or basket for that meal.

3. Gather the young people around the meal or meals, and tell them each to put a hand on a box or basket. Ask them to think about the people who will be eating the meal or meals they built and to imagine what those people might look like. Pause for a moment of silence, then say a short prayer for God's blessings on the builders of the meal or meals and on those who will receive the food.

4. Deliver each meal to its designated family or other location, or ask some of the participants' parents to take care of this task.

ALTERNATIVE APPROACHES

◎ This strategy can become a parishwide project led by the young teens. Planning and publicity for the project will have to start early in the fall. Everyone in the parish can bring food items. The young teens can work with children in the parish to make tablecloths and prayer cards. When everything is collected, the young people can spend one weekend afternoon before the holiday building meals.
◎ Instead of just bringing food items, the young people can do a fund-raiser in the fall to make some money, then go shopping together for the necessary items.
◎ Though Thanksgiving is a logical time for this project, families find themselves in need at all times of the year. Consider doing a meal project at an unusual time, like the Fourth of July, Saint Patrick's Day, or just any month.
◎ In the process of building a meal, discuss with the young people the various reasons why some families may not have adequate food. A lack of food might have to do with the number of people in the household, joblessness, low wages, or any number of other situations. This would be a good chance to talk with the young teens about Catholic social teaching.

SCRIPTURAL CONNECTIONS

◎ Isa. 58:6–9 (Share your bread with the hungry.)
◎ Ezek. 18:5–9 (A just person gives food to the hungry.)
◎ Matt. 25:31–40 (Feed the hungry.)

NOTES

Use the space below to jot notes and reminders for the next time you use this strategy.

Advent Buddies

An Intergenerational Relationship-Building Activity

This activity helps the young people each learn from an older person in the parish and establish a faith relationship with that person.

Suggested Time

About 15 minutes for each meeting during Advent

Group Size

This strategy can be done with any number of young teens, as long as each one can be paired with an older person.

Special Considerations

This activity takes place in separate meetings during Advent and a celebration gathering during the Christmas season. It depends on your consistency in arranging and facilitating those meetings, and on the willingness of older people in the community to make a seasonal commitment to the young people. Well before Advent you will need to personally invite those elders to take part in the activity, and explain the process and the extent of the commitment. Be sure the elders know the following things:

◎ They will each receive a note from a young person in the mail each week during Advent (or as often as you have arranged for the young people to meet). The note will not be signed, and the name of their buddy will not be revealed.

◎ They are expected to write back on a postcard or in a note. Their response should be mailed to you, and their name should appear on the postcard or on the outside of the envelope.

◎ The return card or note must arrive at the church or meeting place by a certain day of the week (or by a certain day before each subsequent meeting of the young people).

◎ They will meet their Advent buddy at a special gathering after Christmas.

Materials Needed

☼ index cards
☼ pens or pencils
☼ stamped postcards, or notepaper and stamped envelopes, four for each young person

PROCEDURE

Preparation. Identify the older people who will participate in this strategy and ensure that they understand their role, as described previously in Special Considerations.

Make up individual index cards, each with the name and address of an older person who has expressed a willingness to participate in the activity.

Decide on pairings between the young people and the older people. Make a master list of those pairings for yourself, so that you can match each response from an elder with its young recipient.

Advent Meeting 1

1. Explain to the young people that during Advent they will each have a secret elder pal, otherwise known as an Advent buddy. Tell them that they will know the name of their elder, but that their elder will not know their name. Give each young person the index card with the name and address of the elder you have assigned to him or her.

2. Give each young person a stamped postcard, or a sheet of notepaper and a stamped envelope, and a pen or pencil. Tell the participants to write a note to their secret elder pal. They are to include information about themselves but not reveal their name.

Direct them to ask their Advent buddy to write back and to answer the question, "Why is the church important to you?" Explain that the older person will mail or deliver the answer to you before your next meeting. Have the young people close their note by asking their Advent buddy for prayers and assuring their buddy of prayers in return.

3. When the young people finish writing, direct them to place their note in their envelope and seal the envelope, if they used notepaper. Tell them to address their postcard or envelope, and give it to you to mail.

Advent Meetings 2 to 4

Each week distribute the responses from the older people and give the young people time to read them. In addition direct the young people to write a note to their elder partner asking a new question provided by you. They could also update their partner on the events of the week and ask for prayer support for something in particular.

You may make up your own questions each week, or use any of the ones listed below:

◎ When and how do you pray?
◎ Who is your favorite saint or holy person? Why?
◎ When were you especially aware of God's presence? Explain.
◎ If you were to draw a picture of God, what would it look like?
◎ What does being part of this church mean to you?
◎ If you could ask God one question, what would it be? Why would you ask it?
◎ If you could change anything about the church, what would it be? Why?

Christmas Season Celebration

Sometime during the Christmas season, invite the older people to come to a celebration where the Advent buddies will meet each other. The young people could plan to do a skit, a prayer service, or a talent show. They might also share one-on-one with their Advent buddy their own answers to the questions they asked in their cards or notes.

ALTERNATIVE APPROACHES

◎ Help the young people prepare a party or dinner for the meeting with the elders. They could bring or make cookies and lemonade or punch. If they decide to do a meal, they might make pancakes for breakfast or spaghetti for dinner.

◎ Before the post-Christmas gathering, arrange for the young people each to make a special gift for their elder. It could be something like a bookmark, a magnet, a frame with a picture of the young teen, or a recording of the young person reading a Christmas story.

◎ If you have more than 15 minutes to devote to this activity each week, invite the young people to comment on their partner's answer and share their own thoughts on the issue, before they write and ask their partner a new question.

◎ Instead of having the buddies correspond on postcards or notepaper, put together an inexpensive journal for each pair, by folding a few standard-size sheets of paper in half and stapling them in the middle. Invite both the young people and the elders to write in their shared journal each week.

NOTES

Use the space below to jot notes and reminders for the next time you use this strategy.

Santa Teen

An Outreach Activity for Christmas

OVERVIEW

In this outreach activity, the young people collect Christmas gifts for young teens who are disadvantaged, generally a group that is overlooked at Christmastime.

Suggested Time

10 to 15 minutes for the planning meeting; 30 to 40 minutes for the wrapping party, or longer, depending on the number of gifts and your plans for delivering them.

Group Size

This strategy can be done with any size group.

Materials Needed

- ☼ newsprint and markers
- ☼ a variety of wrapping materials, including gift boxes of various sizes, Christmas wrapping paper, ribbon, scissors, and cellophane tape
- ☼ removable tags

PROCEDURE

Preparation. Contact a local social-service agency, the Salvation Army, Catholic Charities, or a Christmas giving project to announce that you will have some gifts for young teenagers available for Christmas.

Planning Meeting

1. Introduce the activity by explaining that young teenagers who are on their own or are part of poor families are frequently forgotten at Christmastime. Communities often collect toys for children or gifts for families, but do not address the special wants and needs of young teens. If you have particular stories of disadvantaged young teens that you could share with the group, they might be effective.

2. Ask the young people to brainstorm items that a young teenage girl might like for Christmas. List their ideas on newsprint. Make a similar list of items that a young teenage boy might like. Some of the items could be practical and necessary. Others might simply be fun.

3. Tell the participants about the connection you have made with a service agency. Ask them each to identify one or more items on the list that they have or are willing to buy as a Christmas gift for a young teen who is disadvantaged. Ask them to bring the item or items to the next gathering.

Wrapping Party

1. Provide a variety of wrapping materials. Tell the young people to wrap their gifts and to place on the outside of each package a removable tag that identifies the gift and the gender it is most appropriate for.

2. Deliver the gifts to the agency for distribution. You might invite the young people to help with the delivery and to connect with someone who works with young teenagers who are disadvantaged. That person might be able to share stories and talk about the needs of young teens who are poor.

ALTERNATIVE APPROACHES

◎ This strategy might easily become a parishwide activity. Hold the planning meeting with the young people at the beginning of Advent, and then share the brainstormed list of possible gifts with the parish. Do this sharing in the parish bulletin, or help the young people decorate a "giving tree" with handmade ornaments, each identifying one item from the list. Ask the parish for donations, designate a date by which donations should be delivered, and set up a collection point. Gather the young people on a certain day to wrap, mark, and deliver presents.

◎ Because neither poverty nor special needs are seasonal, this strategy will work at any time of the year. It might be fun for the young teens to do a summer service project and gather for other young teens things like beach towels, sunscreen, sunglasses, tokens for the local pool, sandals, and gift certificates for ice cream.

NOTES

Use the space below to jot notes and reminders for the next time you use this strategy.

Stocking Stuffer Relay

A Prayer-Writing Activity for Christmas

OVERVIEW

This game can be used anytime during the Christmas season as an icebreaker, an introduction to a session on the Christmas story, or a prayer.

Suggested Time

20 to 30 minutes

Group Size

This strategy can be done with any size group, in teams of no more than five people.

Materials Needed

- Christmas stockings, one for every five people
- the following items, one of each for each stocking:
  - a small cross
  - a star
  - a rosary
  - a small box wrapped for Christmas
  - a bell

- the following figures from a nativity set, one of each for each stocking:
  - baby Jesus
  - Mary
  - Joseph
  - a shepherd
  - an angel
  - a king
- newsprint and markers
- masking tape

PROCEDURE

Preparation. For this activity you will need one Christmas stocking for every five participants. Before the young people arrive, put in each stocking one of each of the stocking stuffer items and nativity figures listed in the Materials Needed section. Place the stockings in a line across one end of the meeting room.

1. Gather the participants into small groups of no more than five people. Line the teams up at one end of the room, opposite the Christmas stockings. Explain that the young people are going to work with their team to write a Christmas prayer using items that are in the stocking. Give one person on each team a sheet of newsprint and a marker. Then present the following instructions in your own words:

One member of each team runs up to the team's stocking, removes an item, and takes it back to the team. Together the team members write on the newsprint a one-sentence prayer about that item. The prayer should relate to the Christmas story. For example, if the team gets a bell, its prayer might be one of thanks, such as, "O God, as bells ring out the news that Jesus is born, we thank you for the gift of your Son." Then another person on each team follows the same process, and so forth, until all the items in the stocking have been used. When a team finishes all its prayers, one of its members posts the newsprint.

When you are sure the young people understand the directions, give a signal to begin.

After all the teams have finished, declare the winner, that is, the group that finished its prayers first.

2. Gather the participants and read Luke 2:1–16 and Matt. 2:1–12 aloud to them. Ask the young people to compare those two versions of the Christmas story. Point out that the story as we have generally received it is actually a compilation of what is in the Scriptures and what has simply become oral tradition.

3. Close the session by inviting each group to read aloud the prayers it created in the relay.

ALTERNATIVE APPROACHES

◎ This prayer activity can be done without the relay. Give each team a filled stocking, a sheet of newsprint, and some markers. Tell the teams each to take one item from their stocking at a time and write a one-line prayer about it.

◎ Instead of giving separate teams each a stocking and asking them to work on their own prayer, use just one stocking and divide the participants into as many small groups as you have stocking items. Give the small groups each one item and ask them to write a one-line prayer about it. Combine all the one-line prayers into one complete prayer.

◎ After completing the procedure as it is presented, lead all the teams to combine their prayers into one Christmas prayer. They can group all the prayers about stars into one verse, about shepherds into another, and so forth. Publish the prayer in the parish bulletin or newsletter.

SCRIPTURAL CONNECTIONS

The following scriptural citations identify the only accounts of the birth of Jesus found in the Gospels:

◎ Matt. 2:1–12

◎ Luke 2:1–16

NOTES

Use the space below to jot notes and reminders for the next time you use this strategy.

Posada

A Re-enactment of the Beginning of the Christmas Story

OVERVIEW This activity involves the young people in a Latino custom of re-enacting Mary and Joseph's journey to Bethlehem.

Suggested Time

40 to 60 minutes, depending on the size of the group and the number of homes the group stops at

Group Size

This strategy can be done with any size group, but works best with a group of ten people or less.

Special Considerations

If you have a large group, your challenge will be to find some way to involve everyone. Two of the young people will depict Mary and Joseph. Invite others to become a choir to sing Christmas carols as they move from house to house.

Music is also a way to get the attention of the people at whose houses the group stops. The rest of the group can carry flashlights, and use them as spotlights on Mary and Joseph when they arrive at a house.

Materials Needed

- costumes identifying Mary and Joseph
- lyrics for traditional Christmas songs (optional)
- a Bible

PROCEDURE

Preparation. Before the young people gather, select one of them to represent Mary and another to represent Joseph. Ask the young people who are portraying Mary and Joseph to come in costume. (Either supply the costumes or ask the actors to do so.) Prepare these two participants to play the parts described in step 2 of this activity.

Make arrangements with five people in the neighborhood to take part in the activity. Prepare the first four to reject the group when it approaches them for housing. Ask the last person you visit to host a small party for your group.

Prepare to lead the group in singing traditional Christmas hymns as you move from house to house in procession. Or recruit someone else to take on this role. You may want to provide lyrics for the songs.

If you are unfamiliar with the Posada tradition, you may want to read a book about Latino holiday traditions from your local library, or find information about the tradition on the Internet, in order to prepare to answer questions that the young people might ask.

1. Gather the young people and offer the following information in your own words:

 Latino people have a custom of re-enacting Joseph and Mary's search for a place to stay when Jesus was born. The name for this re-enactment is Posada. The event is usually held on an evening during the week before Christmas. Parish families volunteer their homes as sites for the visit of Mary and Joseph. Sometimes people act out the parts of Mary and Joseph, sometimes they carry statues. Typically the last house they visit offers snacks or a meal to the people who take part in the procession.

Explain that as a group the participants too will walk from house to house, led by Mary and Joseph, searching for a place to stay. Mention that as you move from house to house, the group will sing traditional Christmas carols. Distribute lyrics if you have prepared them. Then read Luke 2:1–7 aloud to the group.

2. Supervise the group as it walks to the house of the first neighbor who has agreed to take part in this activity, singing as you go. Ensure that the young people who are playing Mary and Joseph knock at the door, explain that Mary is about to deliver her baby, and ask if they might stay the night. When the resident answers, "There is no room," lead the processional group in saying loudly: "Let us move on. Surely God will provide." As the group moves to the next house, lead the young people in singing a traditional Christmas hymn. Guide the group in repeating this process with each of the first four houses you have arranged to visit.

3. When Mary and Joseph ask to stay the night at the fifth and last house, the host invites the whole group inside for refreshments. After the refreshments ask someone in the host family to read Luke 2:8–14 aloud to the gathering. Then pray the following prayer:

O God, your faithful followers Mary and Joseph faced rejection even as they did your will. We take courage from them because they did not take no for an answer. Instead they continued to search all of Bethlehem for shelter. They trusted in you, and they found a humble place for Mary to give birth to your Son. May we trust as much and learn from their example. We ask this in the name of the Son, Jesus, whose birth we soon celebrate. Amen.

ALTERNATIVE APPROACHES

◎ Instead of recruiting a Mary and Joseph to dress in costume, provide statues of Mary and Joseph. Then allow different people to carry the statues from house to house and play Mary and Joseph.
◎ If your group includes mostly non-Latino people, invite someone who grew up in a Latino family to talk about their experience of Posada and describe how they celebrated the holiday in their culture.

SCRIPTURAL CONNECTIONS

◎ Mic. 5:1–2 (Little Bethlehem will be the place for the holy birth.)
◎ Luke 2:1–7 (There was no room at the inn.)

NOTES

Use the space below to jot notes and reminders for the next time you use this strategy.

Happy Birthday, Everyone

A Community-Building Activity and Service Event

OVERVIEW This birthday party provides an opportunity for the young teens to help people their age who are not likely to get many presents when their birthday comes around. It also fosters discussion among the young people.

Suggested Time

About 60 minutes, depending on the size of the group and how elaborate the wrapping and card-making process is

Group Size

This strategy can be done with any size group. It works particularly well with large groups.

Materials Needed

- ☼ announcements suggesting that the young people bring a gift
- ☼ balloons, streamers, and other room decorations
- ☼ labels or stickers that say "It's my birthday!," party hats, and noisemakers (optional)
- ☼ newsprint and markers

☼ masking tape
☼ gift wrap (standard wrapping paper, shelf paper, wallpaper, or the color comics from the Sunday newspaper), ribbon, and bows
☼ scissors
☼ cellophane tape
☼ stick-on labels, one for each person
☼ construction paper and a variety of other card-making supplies
☼ a birthday cake and beverages

PROCEDURE

Preparation. Check with local social service agencies for ideas about dispersing the birthday gifts after the party. Be sure the agency is aware that the gifts are intended for young teens.

Before the birthday party, send the young people an announcement about it. Tell them to bring a birthday gift that they would like to receive. You may want to put a price limit on the gift to avoid competition. Tell them to bring their gift unwrapped.

Decorate your meeting space with balloons, streamers, and anything else you can find to create a festive party atmosphere.

Write the following sentence-starters on newsprint. Post the newsprint in your meeting space, and cover it until it is needed.

◎ The three best things about being born in _____ (month or season) are . . .
◎ The three worst things about being born in _____ (month or season) are . . .
◎ Five things that we all have in common are . . .
◎ One thing that is unique about each of us is . . .

1. As everyone arrives greet them with wishes for a happy birthday and direct them to place their gift in a central location. If you have them available, give out "It's my birthday!" labels or stickers, party hats, and noisemakers. Point out that everyone has a birthday one day out of the year, and the purpose of this event is to celebrate the gift of life.

2. Tell the participants to form a single line. Explain that the young people are to arrange their line in order of birthdays, starting with January at one end and ending with December at the other. Ages do not matter. They must arrange themselves *without speaking or mouthing words.*

3. When the young teens have completed their lineup, make sure they are in order by asking everyone to state their birth date. Then lead a discussion around the following questions:

What system did you come up with for finding out birth dates? Whose idea was it?

Did you try any other methods before hitting on the one that worked?

What was the level of co-operation?

How is this activity like what sometimes happens in life?

Close by making these brief comments in your own words:

Just as everyone had a place in their line, each person was born for a distinct purpose. Finding our place in the world is one of the great challenges in life.

Sometimes we have to work around obstacles that are placed before us. In the lineup, the obstacle was not being able to speak. But with some thought and by sharing ideas with one another, we can accomplish what we need to.

It's important to recognize the leaders in a group, because the role of leader may fall to different people at different times. It is also important to be a leader when we are called to do so. Being a leader is part of taking our place in the world.

Cooperation among everyone at all times is the key to getting things done. We need other people in order to succeed, and they need us.

4. Divide the participants into small groups according to birth months or, if you have a small number of participants, according to the four seasons of the year. Give each small group a sheet of newsprint and some markers. Reveal the sentence-starters you posted before the event, and tell the groups each to complete them on their newsprint.

Note that for the sentence-starter about things they have in common, the group members should avoid obvious answers, such as, "We were all born in January" or "We are all in the seventh grade" or "We all go to Saint Cuthburga Church." You may need to give some examples of valid answers to the last sentence-starter, such as, "Victoria was born in New York" or "William's grandfather is a farmer."

Allow about 10 minutes for the groups to work on their answers. (You may need to allow more time if the groups are large.) After the groups finish, invite them to share their newsprint with everyone.

5. Gather the young people in a circle around the gifts they brought, and tell them each to claim their own gift and then sit down. Explain where their gifts will be going and who will receive them. Tell them to look at their gift silently and try to picture the young person who might eventually receive it. Make the following comments in your own words:

The person who will receive the gift you brought is about the same age as you are. You have a lot of things in common with that person, just as you did with the people in your group. Like you that person has hopes, dreams, and fears. That person laughs and cries, wins and loses, celebrates some things and regrets others.

That person also has something that is unique about him or her, just as you do. It may be a special talent, a rare experience, or a secret.

Like all of us, the person who will receive your gift has something special to offer. God created that person to take a particular place in the world. In order to do so, that person needs love, support, encouragement, and an occasional helping hand—just like we all do.

6. Ask everyone to offer for the recipient of their gift a prayer that is a reflection of the gift itself. For example, if the gift is a music CD, the prayer might be that the person find joy in the music. If the gift is a book of jokes, the prayer might be for the gift of laughter. If the gift is makeup, the prayer might be that the person see her inner beauty. If the young people are comfortable doing so, ask them each to share their prayer aloud.

7. Provide gift wrap, ribbon, and bows; scissors; and cellophane tape. Direct the young people each to wrap their gift, and provide stick-on labels so that they can identify the gender and age of the person it is for.

Also supply construction paper and a variety of other materials for making cards. Encourage the participants each to make a birthday card and write in it a greeting and the prayer that they came up with. Have them tape the card to the package.

8. Close the event by singing "Happy Birthday to You" and sharing birthday cake and beverages.

ALTERNATIVE APPROACHES

◎ If you have more than twenty people, divide them into two equal lines in step 2, and add an element of competition.

◎ To make the birthday lineup more challenging, blindfold the participants. To make it even more challenging, direct them to line up (with or without blindfolds) on a bench, on a log, or within two lines on the floor that you mark off with masking tape.

◎ If your budget will allow it, give each person in the group a small birthday gift from the parish. It might be something like a bookmark, a pencil that says "Happy birthday," a pin with a religious symbol, or a smooth rock labeled with their name, their birth date, and the name of the parish.

To extend this session, lead the young people in a variety of mixers and group games. Check out *Creative Crowd-Breakers, Mixers, and Games,* compiled by Wayne Rice and Mike Yaconelli (Winona, MN: Saint Mary's Press, 1991), or the books of games available from Group Publishing (web site *www.grouppublishing.com,* phone 800-447-1070) or Youth Specialties (web site *www.youthspecialties.com,* phone 800-776-8008). Add a birthday twist when you can.

NOTES

Use the space below to jot notes and reminders for the next time you use this strategy.

Holiday Wheel of Fortune

An Icebreaker for Any Holiday

This icebreaker, based on the TV game show *Wheel of Fortune,* can be adapted for use during any holiday or season by changing the name, phrase, or scriptural verse to be identified. It is a helpful way of focusing young teens' attention.

Suggested Time

10 to 15 minutes, depending on the size of the group and the length of the puzzle

Group Size

This icebreaker works well with groups of three to eight people. If you have more participants, assign them to small groups of three to eight.

Materials Needed

- ☼ 3-by-5- or 4-by-6-inch index cards
- ☼ a marker
- ☼ masking tape
- ☼ a pen or pencil
- ☼ a scissors

☼ boxes, baskets, bowls, or bags, two for every puzzle
☼ wrapped candy
☼ small prizes (optional)

PROCEDURE

Preparation. You will need one game puzzle for every three to eight participants (see the discussion under Group Size earlier in this strategy). Depending on the holiday or season you are observing, find a name, phrase, or scriptural verse to use for each puzzle. Suggestions for holiday and seasonal puzzles are as follows:

Valentine's Day
◎ Love one another as I have loved you. [John 15:12]
◎ Love is patient; love is kind. [1 Cor. 13:4]

Saint Patrick's Day
◎ Luck of the Irish
◎ Patron saint of Ireland

Mother's Day or Father's Day
◎ Honor your father and your mother. [Exod. 20:12]
◎ Mary and Joseph

Halloween
◎ Trick or treat
◎ Do not be afraid, for I am with you and will bless you. [Gen. 26:24]

Independence Day
◎ The Declaration of Independence
◎ Thomas Jefferson

Advent
◎ Prepare the way of the Lord. [Matt. 3:3]
◎ A voice cries in the wilderness. [Matt. 3:3]

For each puzzle complete the following tasks:
◎ Write each letter of the name, phrase, or verse on a separate index card. Also write each punctuation mark (such as a comma or hyphen) on a separate card. Do not include the citations given in brackets for the scriptural quotes; those are for your information only.
◎ Tape the cards on a wall in order, leaving spaces between the words. Turn the cards with punctuation marks so that those marks face out. Turn the cards with letters so that the letters face the wall, ensuring that the cards can be turned over to reveal the letters later.
◎ Write the entire phrase, name, or verse for the puzzle on a separate index card.

◎ Cut several index cards into 1-by-2-inch strips. You will need at least twenty strips, but you may use as many strips as you want to. Label the strips as follows:
  ◎ 1 (at least two strips)
  ◎ 2 (at least four strips)
  ◎ 3 (at least four strips)
  ◎ 4 (at least three strips)
  ◎ 5 (at least two strips)
  ◎ 6 (at least one strip)
  ◎ Lose a turn (at least two strips)
  ◎ Bankrupt (at least two strips)
  Put the strips into a box, basket, bowl, or bag, and place the container near the puzzle.
◎ Place a box, basket, bowl, or bag of wrapped candy near the puzzle. If possible, use candy with an appropriate seasonal wrapping.

1. If you have more than eight participants, divide them into small groups as discussed under Group Size near the beginning of this strategy. For each small group, designate someone to be the emcee. You may wish to ask a different person in the group to turn over the puzzle letters, although the emcee can probably cover that task. Assign the other young teens in the group to be contestants, working either alone or in pairs. To keep the game moving, limit the contestants or contestant pairs to no more than three.

2. Show the emcee and letter turner for each group the index card with the group's puzzle written on it. Tell them not to reveal the puzzle to the contestants.

3. Explain the following rules to the young people:

The emcee asks a contestant or pair of contestants to choose one instruction slip from the container near the puzzle and reveal it to the group. Then the contestant or pair calls out a letter. If that letter is included in the puzzle, the contestant or pair gets the number of candies designated on the slip, multiplied by the number of times the letter appears in the puzzle. The contestant or pair may then try to solve the puzzle. If the puzzle is not solved, the emcee moves on to the next contestant or pair. That contestant or pair may either try to solve the puzzle or draw an instruction slip from the container. The play continues in this manner, passing from one contestant or pair to another, until the puzzle is solved.

Contestants may buy vowels at a cost of five candies. They may do so only during their own turn at the puzzle, instead of calling out a letter and before they attempt to solve the puzzle. They may buy only one vowel during a turn.

If a contestant or pair picks a strip that says, "Lose a turn," the contestant or pair may not choose a letter or buy a vowel or try to solve the puzzle; play moves immediately to the next person or pair. If a contestant or pair picks a strip that says, "Bankrupt," the contestant or pair loses all its candies.

The contestant or pair that solves the puzzle first is the winner.

4. When you are sure that the young people understand the rules, start the game. If you have prizes available, award them to the person or pair that correctly solves the puzzle.

ALTERNATIVE APPROACHES

◎ Allow the young teens to create puzzles for one another or for younger children, using appropriate scriptural verses.
◎ Use this activity as part of a game show night during which a variety of game show formats are used to help the young people review material. Other game show formats that work well include *Jeopardy* and *Hollywood Squares*.

NOTES

Use the space below to jot notes and reminders for the next time you use this strategy.

Appendix 1
Connections to the Discovering Program by HELP Strategy

"Getting a Fresh Start: A Reflection Activity on New Year's Resolutions"

As presented, this strategy complements the following Discovering courses:
- ◎ *Making Decisions*
- ◎ *Understanding Myself*

You may also adapt this strategy to fit any course in the Discovering Program by tailoring the nature of the resolution to the topic you are discussing.

"'I Have a Dream': A Reflection Exercise on the Speech by Dr. Martin Luther King Jr."

This strategy may be used with any course in the Discovering Program, especially the following four:
- ◎ *Being Catholic*
- ◎ *Exploring the Story of Israel*
- ◎ *Meeting Jesus*
- ◎ *Seeking Justice*

"Soup or Bowl:
A Game and Service Project for Super Bowl Sunday"

This strategy may be used with any course in the Discovering Program, especially the following two:
- *Being Catholic*
- *Seeking Justice*

"Valentine Visit:
An Outreach Event for Valentine's Day"

This strategy complements the following courses in the Discovering Program:
- *Being Catholic*
- *Meeting Jesus*
- *Seeking Justice*

"Real Love Is . . . : A Community-Building
and Discussion Event for Valentine's Day"

This strategy complements the following courses in the Discovering Program:
- *Becoming Friends*
- *Learning to Communicate*
- *Praying*
- *Understanding Myself*

"Ashes to Reconciliation:
A Reconciliation Prayer for Lent"

This strategy may be used with any course in the Discovering Program that is taught during Lent. It is especially appropriate to the following three:
- *Being Catholic*
- *Gathering to Celebrate*
- *Praying*

"Lenten Nails: A Reflection Exercise for Lent"

This strategy may be used with any course in the Discovering Program, especially the following three:
- *Being Catholic*
- *Gathering to Celebrate*
- *Praying*

"Justice Walk:
A Contemporary Version of the Stations of the Cross"

This strategy may be used with any course in the Discovering Program, especially the following four:
◎ *Being Catholic*
◎ *Meeting Jesus*
◎ *Praying*
◎ *Seeking Justice*

"The Passion Here and Now:
A Contemporary Look at the Passion of Jesus Christ"

This strategy complements the following courses in the Discovering Program:
◎ *Exploring the Bible*
◎ *Meeting Jesus*
◎ *Seeking Justice*

"Resurrection Relay:
A Bible Learning Activity for Easter"

This strategy complements the following Discovering courses:
◎ *Exploring the Bible*
◎ *Meeting Jesus*

"Be a Fool for Christ:
A Prayer Service for April Fools' Day"

This strategy complements the following courses in the Discovering Program:
◎ *Making Decisions*
◎ *Meeting Jesus*
◎ *Seeking Justice*

"Mary, Full of Grace:
A Learning Activity for the Month of May"

This strategy complements the following Discovering course:
◎ *Being Catholic*

"The Spirit Blows: A Hands-on Activity for Pentecost"

This strategy complements the following Discovering courses:

- *Being Catholic*
- *Exploring the Bible*
- *Seeking Justice*
- *Understanding Myself*

"Tower of Independence: A Discussion Activity for Independence Day"

This strategy complements the following Discovering courses:

- *Becoming Friends*
- *Dealing with Tough Times*
- *Making Decisions*
- *Understanding Myself*

"TGIS (Thank God It's Summer)! An End-of-School Celebration"

This strategy may be used at the end of a school year and beginning of summer. It has no connection to any specific course or courses in the Discovering Program.

"Back-to-School Blessing: A Prayer Service for the Beginning of the School Year"

This strategy may be used with any course in the Discovering Program. It should be combined with the first course that is offered at the beginning of the school year.

"Fears: A Discussion Exercise for Halloween"

This strategy complements the following Discovering courses:

- *Dealing with Tough Times*
- *Understanding Myself*

"Trick-or-Treat for a Cause: An Outreach Activity for Halloween"

This strategy may be used with any course in the Discovering Program, especially the following two:

- *Being Catholic*
- *Seeking Justice*

"Unmasking Saints: A Learning Activity for All Saints' Day"

This strategy complements the following courses in the Discovering Program:
- *Being Catholic*
- *Seeking Justice*

"Giving Thanks for Special People: A Communication Activity for Thanksgiving"

This strategy may be used with any course in the Discovering Program.

"Build a Meal: An Outreach Activity for Thanksgiving"

This strategy may be used with any course in the Discovering Program. It has particular application to the following courses:
- *Being Catholic*
- *Seeking Justice*

"Advent Buddies: An Intergenerational Relationship-Building Activity"

This strategy may be used with any course in the Discovering Program.

"Santa Teen: An Outreach Activity for Christmas"

This strategy may be used with any course in the Discovering Program, especially the following two:
- *Being Catholic*
- *Seeking Justice*

"Stocking Stuffer Relay: A Prayer-Writing Activity for Christmas"

This strategy complements the following Discovering courses:
- *Being Catholic*
- *Meeting Jesus*
- *Praying*

"Posada: A Re-enactment of the Beginning of the Christmas Story"

This strategy complements the following courses in the Discovering Program:
- ◎ *Being Catholic*
- ◎ *Meeting Jesus*

"Happy Birthday, Everyone: A Community-Building Activity and Service Event"

This strategy may be used with any course in the Discovering Program, especially the following four:
- ◎ *Becoming Friends*
- ◎ *Gathering to Celebrate*
- ◎ *Seeking Justice*
- ◎ *Understanding Myself*

"Holiday Wheel of Fortune: An Icebreaker for Any Holiday"

This strategy may be used with any course in the Discovering Program.

Appendix 2

Connections to the Discovering Program by Discovering Course

Becoming Friends

The following HELP strategy is especially suited for use with this course:
◎ "Happy Birthday, Everyone: A Community-Building Activity and Service Event"

These HELP strategies also complement this course as they are presented:
◎ "'I Have a Dream': A Reflection Exercise on the Speech by Dr. Martin Luther King Jr."
◎ "Soup or Bowl: A Game and Service Project for Super Bowl Sunday"
◎ "Real Love Is . . . : A Community-Building and Discussion Event for Valentine's Day"
◎ "Lenten Nails: A Reflection Exercise for Lent"
◎ "Justice Walk: A Contemporary Version of the Stations of the Cross"
◎ "Tower of Independence: A Discussion Activity for Independence Day"
◎ "Back-to-School Blessing: A Prayer Service for the Beginning of the School Year" (This strategy should be combined with the first course that is offered at the beginning of the school year.)
◎ "Trick-or-Treat for a Cause: An Outreach Activity for Halloween"

- "Giving Thanks for Special People: A Communication Activity for Thanksgiving"
- "Build a Meal: An Outreach Activity for Thanksgiving"
- "Advent Buddies: An Intergenerational Relationship-Building Activity"
- "Santa Teen: An Outreach Activity for Christmas"
- "Holiday Wheel of Fortune: An Icebreaker for Any Holiday"

The HELP strategy listed here may be adapted for use with this course by tailoring the nature of the resolution to the topic you are discussing:
- "Getting a Fresh Start: A Reflection Activity on New Year's Resolutions"

The following HELP strategy is not connected to this course by theme but may be used with it at the end of the school year and the beginning of summer:
- "TGIS (Thank God It's Summer)! An End-of-School Celebration"

The HELP strategy listed below may be used with this course if it is taught during Lent:
- "Ashes to Reconciliation: A Reconciliation Prayer for Lent"

Being Catholic

The following HELP strategies are especially suited for use with this course:
- "'I Have a Dream': A Reflection Exercise on the Speech by Dr. Martin Luther King Jr."
- "Soup or Bowl: A Game and Service Project for Super Bowl Sunday"
- "Ashes to Reconciliation: A Reconciliation Prayer for Lent"
- "Lenten Nails: A Reflection Exercise for Lent"
- "Justice Walk: A Contemporary Version of the Stations of the Cross"
- "Trick-or-Treat for a Cause: An Outreach Activity for Halloween"
- "Build a Meal: An Outreach Activity for Thanksgiving"
- "Santa Teen: An Outreach Activity for Christmas"

These HELP strategies also complement this course as they are presented:
- "Valentine Visit: An Outreach Event for Valentine's Day"
- "Mary, Full of Grace: A Learning Activity for the Month of May"
- "The Spirit Blows: Hands-on Activity for Pentecost"
- "Back-to-School Blessing: A Prayer Service for the Beginning of the School Year" (This strategy should be combined with the first course that is offered at the beginning of the school year.)
- "Unmasking Saints: A Learning Activity for All Saints' Day"
- "Giving Thanks for Special People: A Communication Activity for Thanksgiving"
- "Advent Buddies: An Intergenerational Relationship-Building Activity"
- "Stocking Stuffer Relay: A Prayer-Writing Activity for Christmas"
- "Posada: A Re-enactment of the Beginning of the Christmas Story"

- ◎ "Happy Birthday, Everyone: A Community-Building Activity and Service Event"
- ◎ "Holiday Wheel of Fortune: An Icebreaker for Any Holiday"

The HELP strategy listed here may be adapted for use with this course by tailoring the nature of the resolution to the topic you are discussing:
- ◎ "Getting a Fresh Start: A Reflection Activity on New Year's Resolutions"

The following HELP strategy is not connected to this course by theme but may be used with it at the end of the school year and the beginning of summer:
- ◎ "TGIS (Thank God It's Summer)! An End-of-School Celebration"

Celebrating the Eucharist

These HELP strategies complement this course as they are presented:
- ◎ "'I Have a Dream': A Reflection Exercise on the Speech by Dr. Martin Luther King Jr."
- ◎ "Soup or Bowl: A Game and Service Project for Super Bowl Sunday"
- ◎ "Lenten Nails: A Reflection Exercise for Lent"
- ◎ "Justice Walk: A Contemporary Version of the Stations of the Cross"
- ◎ "Back-to-School Blessing: A Prayer Service for the Beginning of the School Year" (This strategy should be combined with the first course that is offered at the beginning of the school year.)
- ◎ "Trick-or-Treat for a Cause: An Outreach Activity for Halloween"
- ◎ "Giving Thanks for Special People: A Communication Activity for Thanksgiving"
- ◎ "Build a Meal: An Outreach Activity for Thanksgiving"
- ◎ "Advent Buddies: An Intergenerational Relationship-Building Activity"
- ◎ "Santa Teen: An Outreach Activity for Christmas"
- ◎ "Happy Birthday, Everyone: A Community-Building Activity and Service Event"
- ◎ "Holiday Wheel of Fortune: An Icebreaker for Any Holiday"

The HELP strategy listed here may be adapted for use with this course by tailoring the nature of the resolution to the topic you are discussing:
- ◎ "Getting a Fresh Start: A Reflection Activity on New Year's Resolutions"

The following HELP strategy is not connected to this course by theme but may be used with it at the end of the school year and the beginning of summer:
- ◎ "TGIS (Thank God It's Summer)! An End-of-School Celebration"

The HELP strategy listed below may be used with this course if it is taught during Lent:
- ◎ "Ashes to Reconciliation: A Reconciliation Prayer for Lent"

Dealing with Tough Times

These HELP strategies complement this course as they are presented:
- "'I Have a Dream': A Reflection Exercise on the Speech by Dr. Martin Luther King Jr."
- "Soup or Bowl: A Game and Service Project for Super Bowl Sunday"
- "Lenten Nails: A Reflection Exercise for Lent"
- "Justice Walk: A Contemporary Version of the Stations of the Cross"
- "Tower of Independence: A Discussion Activity for Independence Day"
- "Back-to-School Blessing: A Prayer Service for the Beginning of the School Year" (This strategy should be combined with the first course that is offered at the beginning of the school year.)
- "Fears: A Discussion Exercise for Halloween"
- "Trick-or-Treat for a Cause: An Outreach Activity for Halloween"
- "Giving Thanks for Special People: A Communication Activity for Thanksgiving"
- "Build a Meal: An Outreach Activity for Thanksgiving"
- "Advent Buddies: An Intergenerational Relationship-Building Activity"
- "Santa Teen: An Outreach Activity for Christmas"
- "Happy Birthday, Everyone: A Community-Building Activity and Service Event"
- "Holiday Wheel of Fortune: An Icebreaker for Any Holiday"

The HELP strategy listed here may be adapted for use with this course by tailoring the nature of the resolution to the topic you are discussing:
- "Getting a Fresh Start: A Reflection Activity on New Year's Resolutions"

The following HELP strategy is not connected to this course by theme but may be used with it at the end of the school year and the beginning of summer:
- "TGIS (Thank God It's Summer)! An End-of-School Celebration"

The HELP strategy listed below may be used with this course if it is taught during Lent:
- "Ashes to Reconciliation: A Reconciliation Prayer for Lent"

Exploring the Bible

These HELP strategies complement this course as they are presented:
- "'I Have a Dream': A Reflection Exercise on the Speech by Dr. Martin Luther King Jr."
- "Soup or Bowl: A Game and Service Project for Super Bowl Sunday"
- "Lenten Nails: A Reflection Exercise for Lent"
- "Justice Walk: A Contemporary Version of the Stations of the Cross"
- "The Passion Here and Now: A Contemporary Look at the Passion of Jesus Christ"

- ☺ "Resurrection Relay: A Bible Learning Activity for Easter"
- ☺ "The Spirit Blows: Hands-on Activity for Pentecost"
- ☺ "Back-to-School Blessing: A Prayer Service for the Beginning of the School Year" (This strategy should be combined with the first course that is offered at the beginning of the school year.)
- ☺ "Trick-or-Treat for a Cause: An Outreach Activity for Halloween"
- ☺ "Giving Thanks for Special People: A Communication Activity for Thanksgiving"
- ☺ "Build a Meal: An Outreach Activity for Thanksgiving"
- ☺ "Advent Buddies: An Intergenerational Relationship-Building Activity"
- ☺ "Santa Teen: An Outreach Activity for Christmas"
- ☺ "Happy Birthday, Everyone: A Community-Building Activity and Service Event"
- ☺ "Holiday Wheel of Fortune: An Icebreaker for Any Holiday"

The HELP strategy listed here may be adapted for use with this course by tailoring the nature of the resolution to the topic you are discussing:
- ☺ "Getting a Fresh Start: A Reflection Activity on New Year's Resolutions"

The following HELP strategy is not connected to this course by theme but may be used with it at the end of the school year and the beginning of summer:
- ☺ "TGIS (Thank God It's Summer)! An End-of-School Celebration"

The HELP strategy listed below may be used with this course if it is taught during Lent:
- ☺ "Ashes to Reconciliation: A Reconciliation Prayer for Lent"

Exploring the Story of Israel

The following HELP strategy is especially suited for use with this course:
- ☺ "'I Have a Dream': A Reflection Exercise on the Speech by Dr. Martin Luther King Jr."

These HELP strategies also complement this course as they are presented:
- ☺ "Soup or Bowl: A Game and Service Project for Super Bowl Sunday"
- ☺ "Lenten Nails: A Reflection Exercise for Lent"
- ☺ "Justice Walk: A Contemporary Version of the Stations of the Cross"
- ☺ "Back-to-School Blessing: A Prayer Service for the Beginning of the School Year" (This strategy should be combined with the first course that is offered at the beginning of the school year.)
- ☺ "Trick-or-Treat for a Cause: An Outreach Activity for Halloween"
- ☺ "Giving Thanks for Special People: A Communication Activity for Thanksgiving"
- ☺ "Build a Meal: An Outreach Activity for Thanksgiving"
- ☺ "Advent Buddies: An Intergenerational Relationship-Building Activity"

◎ "Santa Teen: An Outreach Activity for Christmas"
◎ "Happy Birthday, Everyone: A Community-Building Activity and Service Event"
◎ "Holiday Wheel of Fortune: An Icebreaker for Any Holiday"

The HELP strategy listed here may be adapted for use with this course by tailoring the nature of the resolution to the topic you are discussing:
◎ "Getting a Fresh Start: A Reflection Activity on New Year's Resolutions"

The following HELP strategy is not connected to this course by theme but may be used with it at the end of the school year and the beginning of summer:
◎ "TGIS (Thank God It's Summer)! An End-of-School Celebration"

The HELP strategy listed below may be used with this course if it is taught during Lent:
◎ "Ashes to Reconciliation: A Reconciliation Prayer for Lent"

Gathering to Celebrate

The following HELP strategies are especially suited for use with this course:
◎ "Ashes to Reconciliation: A Reconciliation Prayer for Lent"
◎ "Lenten Nails: A Reflection Exercise for Lent"
◎ "Happy Birthday, Everyone: A Community-Building Activity and Service Event"

These HELP strategies also complement this course as they are presented:
◎ "'I Have a Dream': A Reflection Exercise on the Speech by Dr. Martin Luther King Jr."
◎ "Soup or Bowl: A Game and Service Project for Super Bowl Sunday"
◎ "Justice Walk: A Contemporary Version of the Stations of the Cross"
◎ "Back-to-School Blessing: A Prayer Service for the Beginning of the School Year" (This strategy should be combined with the first course that is offered at the beginning of the school year.)
◎ "Trick-or-Treat for a Cause: An Outreach Activity for Halloween"
◎ "Giving Thanks for Special People: A Communication Activity for Thanksgiving"
◎ "Build a Meal: An Outreach Activity for Thanksgiving"
◎ "Advent Buddies: An Intergenerational Relationship-Building Activity"
◎ "Santa Teen: An Outreach Activity for Christmas"
◎ "Holiday Wheel of Fortune: An Icebreaker for Any Holiday"

The HELP strategy listed here may be adapted for use with this course by tailoring the nature of the resolution to the topic you are discussing:
◎ "Getting a Fresh Start: A Reflection Activity on New Year's Resolutions"

The following HELP strategy is not connected to this course by theme but may be used with it at the end of the school year and the beginning of summer:
- "TGIS (Thank God It's Summer)! An End-of-School Celebration"

Growing Up Sexually

These HELP strategies complement this course as they are presented:
- "'I Have a Dream': A Reflection Exercise on the Speech by Dr. Martin Luther King Jr."
- "Soup or Bowl: A Game and Service Project for Super Bowl Sunday"
- "Lenten Nails: A Reflection Exercise for Lent"
- "Justice Walk: A Contemporary Version of the Stations of the Cross"
- "Back-to-School Blessing: A Prayer Service for the Beginning of the School Year" (This strategy should be combined with the first course that is offered at the beginning of the school year.)
- "Trick-or-Treat for a Cause: An Outreach Activity for Halloween"
- "Giving Thanks for Special People: A Communication Activity for Thanksgiving"
- "Build a Meal: An Outreach Activity for Thanksgiving"
- "Advent Buddies: An Intergenerational Relationship-Building Activity"
- "Santa Teen: An Outreach Activity for Christmas"
- "Happy Birthday, Everyone: A Community-Building Activity and Service Event"
- "Holiday Wheel of Fortune: An Icebreaker for Any Holiday"

The HELP strategy listed here may be adapted for use with this course by tailoring the nature of the resolution to the topic you are discussing:
- "Getting a Fresh Start: A Reflection Activity on New Year's Resolutions"

The following HELP strategy is not connected to this course by theme but may be used with it at the end of the school year and the beginning of summer:
- "TGIS (Thank God It's Summer)! An End-of-School Celebration"

The HELP strategy listed below may be used with this course if it is taught during Lent:
- "Ashes to Reconciliation: A Reconciliation Prayer for Lent"

Learning to Communicate

These HELP strategies complement this course as they are presented:
- "'I Have a Dream': A Reflection Exercise on the Speech by Dr. Martin Luther King Jr."
- "Soup or Bowl: A Game and Service Project for Super Bowl Sunday"

◎ "Real Love Is . . . : A Community-Building and Discussion Event for Valentine's Day"

◎ "Lenten Nails: A Reflection Exercise for Lent"

◎ "Justice Walk: A Contemporary Version of the Stations of the Cross"

◎ "Back-to-School Blessing: A Prayer Service for the Beginning of the School Year" (This strategy should be combined with the first course that is offered at the beginning of the school year.)

◎ "Trick-or-Treat for a Cause: An Outreach Activity for Halloween"

◎ "Giving Thanks for Special People: A Communication Activity for Thanksgiving"

◎ "Build a Meal: An Outreach Activity for Thanksgiving"

◎ "Advent Buddies: An Intergenerational Relationship-Building Activity"

◎ "Santa Teen: An Outreach Activity for Christmas"

◎ "Happy Birthday, Everyone: A Community-Building Activity and Service Event"

◎ "Holiday Wheel of Fortune: An Icebreaker for Any Holiday"

The HELP strategy listed here may be adapted for use with this course by tailoring the nature of the resolution to the topic you are discussing:

◎ "Getting a Fresh Start: A Reflection Activity on New Year's Resolutions"

The following HELP strategy is not connected to this course by theme but may be used with it at the end of the school year and the beginning of summer:

◎ "TGIS (Thank God It's Summer)! An End-of-School Celebration"

The HELP strategy listed below may be used with this course if it is taught during Lent:

◎ "Ashes to Reconciliation: A Reconciliation Prayer for Lent"

Making Decisions

These HELP strategies complement this course as they are presented:

◎ "Getting a Fresh Start: A Reflection Activity on New Year's Resolutions"

◎ "'I Have a Dream': A Reflection Exercise on the Speech by Dr. Martin Luther King Jr."

◎ "Soup or Bowl: A Game and Service Project for Super Bowl Sunday"

◎ "Lenten Nails: A Reflection Exercise for Lent"

◎ "Justice Walk: A Contemporary Version of the Stations of the Cross"

◎ "Be a Fool for Christ: A Prayer Service for April Fools' Day"

◎ "Tower of Independence: A Discussion Activity for Independence Day"

◎ "Back-to-School Blessing: A Prayer Service for the Beginning of the School Year" (This strategy should be combined with the first course that is offered at the beginning of the school year.)

◎ "Trick-or-Treat for a Cause: An Outreach Activity for Halloween"

- "Giving Thanks for Special People: A Communication Activity for Thanks-giving"
- "Build a Meal: An Outreach Activity for Thanksgiving"
- "Advent Buddies: An Intergenerational Relationship-Building Activity"
- "Santa Teen: An Outreach Activity for Christmas"
- "Happy Birthday, Everyone: A Community-Building Activity and Service Event"
- "Holiday Wheel of Fortune: An Icebreaker for Any Holiday"

The following HELP strategy is not connected to this course by theme but may be used with it at the end of the school year and the beginning of summer:
- "TGIS (Thank God It's Summer)! An End-of-School Celebration"

The HELP strategy listed below may be used with this course if it is taught during Lent:
- "Ashes to Reconciliation: A Reconciliation Prayer for Lent"

Meeting Jesus

The following HELP strategies are especially suited for use with this course:
- "'I Have a Dream': A Reflection Exercise on the Speech by Dr. Martin Luther King Jr."
- "Justice Walk: A Contemporary Version of the Stations of the Cross"

These HELP strategies also complement this course as they are presented:
- "Soup or Bowl: A Game and Service Project for Super Bowl Sunday"
- "Valentine Visit: An Outreach Event for Valentine's Day"
- "Lenten Nails: A Reflection Exercise for Lent"
- "The Passion Here and Now: A Contemporary Look at the Passion of Jesus Christ"
- "Resurrection Relay: A Bible Learning Activity for Easter"
- "Be a Fool for Christ: A Prayer Service for April Fools' Day"
- "Back-to-School Blessing: A Prayer Service for the Beginning of the School Year" (This strategy should be combined with the first course that is offered at the beginning of the school year.)
- "Trick-or-Treat for a Cause: An Outreach Activity for Halloween"
- "Giving Thanks for Special People: A Communication Activity for Thanks-giving"
- "Build a Meal: An Outreach Activity for Thanksgiving"
- "Advent Buddies: An Intergenerational Relationship-Building Activity"
- "Santa Teen: An Outreach Activity for Christmas"
- "Stocking Stuffer Relay: A Prayer-Writing Activity for Christmas"
- "Posada: A Re-enactment of the Beginning of the Christmas Story"

◎ "Happy Birthday, Everyone: A Community-Building Activity and Service Event"

◎ "Holiday Wheel of Fortune: An Icebreaker for Any Holiday"

The HELP strategy listed here may be adapted for use with this course by tailoring the nature of the resolution to the topic you are discussing:

◎ "Getting a Fresh Start: A Reflection Activity on New Year's Resolutions"

The following HELP strategy is not connected to this course by theme but may be used with it at the end of the school year and the beginning of summer:

◎ "TGIS (Thank God It's Summer)! An End-of-School Celebration"

The HELP strategy listed below may be used with this course if it is taught during Lent:

◎ "Ashes to Reconciliation: A Reconciliation Prayer for Lent"

Praying

The following HELP strategies are especially suited for use with this course:

◎ "Ashes to Reconciliation: A Reconciliation Prayer for Lent"

◎ "Lenten Nails: A Reflection Exercise for Lent"

◎ "Justice Walk: A Contemporary Version of the Stations of the Cross"

These HELP strategies also complement this course as they are presented:

◎ "'I Have a Dream': A Reflection Exercise on the Speech by Dr. Martin Luther King Jr."

◎ "Soup or Bowl: A Game and Service Project for Super Bowl Sunday"

◎ "Real Love Is . . . : A Community-Building and Discussion Event for Valentine's Day"

◎ "Back-to-School Blessing: A Prayer Service for the Beginning of the School Year" (This strategy should be combined with the first course that is offered at the beginning of the school year.)

◎ "Trick-or-Treat for a Cause: An Outreach Activity for Halloween"

◎ "Giving Thanks for Special People: A Communication Activity for Thanksgiving"

◎ "Build a Meal: An Outreach Activity for Thanksgiving"

◎ "Advent Buddies: An Intergenerational Relationship-Building Activity"

◎ "Santa Teen: An Outreach Activity for Christmas"

◎ "Stocking Stuffer Relay: A Prayer-Writing Activity for Christmas"

◎ "Happy Birthday, Everyone: A Community-Building Activity and Service Event"

◎ "Holiday Wheel of Fortune: An Icebreaker for Any Holiday"

The HELP strategy listed here may be adapted for use with this course by tailoring the nature of the resolution to the topic you are discussing:
◎ "Getting a Fresh Start: A Reflection Activity on New Year's Resolutions"

The following HELP strategy is not connected to this course by theme but may be used with it at the end of the school year and the beginning of summer:
◎ "TGIS (Thank God It's Summer)! An End-of-School Celebration"

Seeking Justice

The following HELP strategies are especially suited for use with this course:
◎ "'I Have a Dream': A Reflection Exercise on the Speech by Dr. Martin Luther King Jr."
◎ "Soup or Bowl: A Game and Service Project for Super Bowl Sunday"
◎ "Justice Walk: A Contemporary Version of the Stations of the Cross"
◎ "Trick-or-Treat for a Cause: An Outreach Activity for Halloween"
◎ "Build a Meal: An Outreach Activity for Thanksgiving"
◎ "Santa Teen: An Outreach Activity for Christmas"
◎ "Happy Birthday, Everyone: A Community-Building Activity and Service Event"

These HELP strategies also complement this course as they are presented:
◎ "Valentine Visit: An Outreach Event for Valentine's Day"
◎ "Lenten Nails: A Reflection Exercise for Lent"
◎ "The Passion Here and Now: A Contemporary Look at the Passion of Jesus Christ"
◎ "Be a Fool for Christ: A Prayer Service for April Fools' Day"
◎ "The Spirit Blows: A Hands-on Activity for Pentecost"
◎ "Back-to-School Blessing: A Prayer Service for the Beginning of the School Year" (This strategy should be combined with the first course that is offered at the beginning of the school year.)
◎ "Unmasking Saints: A Learning Activity for All Saints' Day"
◎ "Giving Thanks for Special People: A Communication Activity for Thanksgiving"
◎ "Advent Buddies: An Intergenerational Relationship-Building Activity"
◎ "Holiday Wheel of Fortune: An Icebreaker for Any Holiday"

The HELP strategy listed here may be adapted for use with this course by tailoring the nature of the resolution to the topic you are discussing:
◎ "Getting a Fresh Start: A Reflection Activity on New Year's Resolutions"

The following HELP strategy is not connected to this course by theme but may be used with it at the end of the school year and the beginning of summer:
◎ "TGIS (Thank God It's Summer)! An End-of-School Celebration"

The HELP strategy listed below may be used with this course if it is taught during Lent:

◎ "Ashes to Reconciliation: A Reconciliation Prayer for Lent"

Understanding Myself

The following HELP strategy is especially suited for use with this course:

◎ "Happy Birthday, Everyone: A Community-Building Activity and Service Event

These HELP strategies also complement this course as they are presented:

◎ "Getting a Fresh Start: A Reflection Activity on New Year's Resolutions"
◎ "'I Have a Dream': A Reflection Exercise on the Speech by Dr. Martin Luther King Jr."
◎ "Soup or Bowl: A Game and Service Project for Super Bowl Sunday"
◎ "Real Love Is . . . : A Community-Building and Discussion Event for Valentine's Day"
◎ "Lenten Nails: A Reflection Exercise for Lent"
◎ "Justice Walk: A Contemporary Version of the Stations of the Cross"
◎ "The Spirit Blows: A Hands-on Activity for Pentecost"
◎ "Tower of Independence: A Discussion Activity for Independence Day"
◎ "Back-to-School Blessing: A Prayer Service for the Beginning of the School Year" (This strategy should be combined with the first course that is offered at the beginning of the school year.)
◎ "Fears: A Discussion Exercise for Halloween"
◎ "Trick-or-Treat for a Cause: An Outreach Activity for Halloween"
◎ "Giving Thanks for Special People: A Communication Activity for Thanksgiving"
◎ "Build a Meal: An Outreach Activity for Thanksgiving"
◎ "Advent Buddies: An Intergenerational Relationship-Building Activity"
◎ "Santa Teen: An Outreach Activity for Christmas"
◎ "Holiday Wheel of Fortune: An Icebreaker for Any Holiday"

The following HELP strategy is not connected to this course by theme but may be used with it at the end of the school year and the beginning of summer:

◎ "TGIS (Thank God It's Summer)! An End-of-School Celebration"

The HELP strategy listed below may be used with this course if it is taught during Lent:

◎ "Ashes to Reconciliation: A Reconciliation Prayer for Lent"

Acknowledgments *(continued)*